The Book of Gratitudes

The Book of Gratitudes

An Encounter between Life and Faith

PABLO R. ANDIÑACH

WIPF & STOCK · Eugene, Oregon

THE BOOK OF GRATITUDES
An Encounter between Life and Faith

Copyright © 2016 Pablo R. Andiñach. All rights reserved. Except for brief quotations in critical publications or reviews, no part of this book may be reproduced in any manner without prior written permission from the publisher. Write: Permissions, Wipf and Stock Publishers, 199 W. 8th Ave., Suite 3, Eugene, OR 97401.

Resource Publications
An Imprint of Wipf and Stock Publishers
199 W. 8th Ave., Suite 3
Eugene, OR 97401

www.wipfandstock.com

PAPERBACK ISBN: 978-1-5326-0788-2
HARDCOVER ISBN: 978-1-5326-0790-5
EBOOK ISBN: 978-1-5326-0789-9

Manufactured in the U.S.A. 12/22/16

Contents

Opening Remarks | ix
For the English Edition | x

Inhabitants of the Pleistocene | 1
In the Beginning, Those Words | 3
Getting One's Bearings in the World | 5
Dry Bones | 7
Names | 9
The Female Disciples | 11
Year One | 13
The Crying Child | 15
Charles Darwin, God and Primates | 17
The Elamite at Pentecost | 19
More Names | 21
Christopher Columbus and the Bible | 23
A Love Story: Jacob and Rachel | 25
Albert Schweitzer or Reverence for Life | 27
Beethoven and the Ninth Symphony | 29
Psalm 8 | 31
The Apostle Julia | 33
Casiodoro de Reina, Bible Translator | 35
The Bible of the Bear | 37
The Bible of the Jar, the Reina-Valera | 40
End of the Reformation in Seville, Spain | 42
The Homunculus and Don Juan Ginés de Sepúlveda | 45

Contents

The Land of the Wichis | 47
Jorgelina Lozada, Woman and Pastor | 49
Sri Lanka or Buenos Aires | 51
The Old Testament Languages | 53
The Koiné Greek of the New Testament | 55
The Septuagint and the Letter of Aristeas | 57
Dinah, the Curious | 59
The First Passover | 61
The First Coin | 63
Mary David Allen, the Birth | 65
Martin Luther King, Your Dream, Our Dream | 67
The Ten Commandments | 69
Delilah, the Woman Samson Loved | 72
Another Love Story: Rebekah and Isaac | 74
Huldah, the Prophetess | 76
The Days from October 5 to 14, 1582 Do Not Exist | 78
The Year in Which We Live | 80
The Origin of Writing | 82
The Hebrew Letters and Their Predecessors | 84
Our Alphabet: From the Phoenicians to Our Times | 86
Luke, the Writer | 88
Jewish Wisdom I | 90
Jewish Wisdom II | 91
Jewish Wisdom III | 92
Jewish Wisdom IV | 93
Sex and the Bible I | 94
Sex and the Bible II | 96
The Apostle Paul | 98
The Mishnah and the Talmud | 100
Psalms, the Bible Hymnbook | 102
Alberto Ricciardi (1922–1999) | 104
The Library | 106
The Bible and First Things | 109
Martha of Bethany, the Invisible | 110
The Junkyard or the Rebirth of the Lost | 112
The Voice of Antonio Porchia | 114

Contents

Jorge Luis Borges and the Infamous Preacher | 116
Evangelina Rodríguez | 118
William C. Morris, Living at Dawn | 120
The Armenian Alphabet | 122
Martin Luther | 124
Far Away and Long Ago | 126
Authors | 128
Uriah, the Murdered Prophet | 130
Nelson Mandela | 132
Stephen or the Hurricane of Words | 134
Of the Origin of Chapters and Verses | 136
Don José and Doña Josefa | 138
Adán Buenosayres, Thoughts on Graves | 140
Cain and Abel | 141
Juana Manso, the Feminist Teacher | 142
Julie Adelaide Hope, a teacher in Paraná | 144
Dirk Henry Kloosterman | 146
The Bandoneon, Birth and Destiny | 148
The Islam | 150
The Koran | 152
Moby Dick, the White Whale | 154
Music and Dance | 156
Rabbi Regina Jonas (1902–1944) | 158
Elohim, Elohai, Allah, God | 160
The National Constitution, Article 15 | 162
The Bible and Slavery | 164
John Wesley | 166
Sophia Campbell and Mary Alley, Slaves | 168
The Crucified God | 170
When Does Day Begin? | 172
Job and the Living Redeemer | 174
That Bread and that Wine | 176
All Loves Excelling | 177

vii

Opening Remarks

THE MONOTONY OF THE Biblical scriptures where one person begat another, and that one another one, and so on and so forth, reveals that no one was made alone and that we all come from, and to a great degree owe what we are, to those who came before us. Just as the Elamite believed he was discovering new words in Pentecost, when they had actually come from the depths of his history, so these pages have some pretense of originality, but are nothing more than bringing to light what we have taken from so many different sources. For this reason, the reader is holding a book full of gratitude. The characters, readings and places that appear in these tales, are the visible components of many others that remain in the dark. I have put into writing only a few, but I dedicate these pages to them all.

P. R. A

For the English Edition

I WANT TO THANKS my colleague Dr. Hugo Magallanes, Director of the Center for the Study of Latino/a Christianity and Religions at Perkins School of Theology, Southern Methodist University in Dallas, Texas, and The Henry Luce Foundation for the grant which allowed the translation and edition of this book. My special thanks to Dr. William Lawrence, former Dean, colleague in ministry and friend for his support and enthusiasm for the edition of this book in English. I want to thanks the translator Elda Bedford who made a marvelous and careful work on a difficult text. And my very special gratitude to my friend Ruth Ramanauskas who read the book, made plenty of style suggestions and translated "The Crucified God," "Julie Adelaide Hope, a Teacher in Paraná" and "The Land of the Wichis." Through her comments and sensitive reading the text has improved its quality and became more beautiful and clear.

P. R. A

Inhabitants of the Pleistocene

HUMAN BEINGS ARE INHABITANTS of the Pleistocene Age or, if we wish to be more precise, the Holocene Era. Anthropology tells us that the *Homo* species became what we now call *Homo sapiens* some two hundred thousand years ago. This "claiming to know"—this is what the word *sapiens* means—should not keep us from reflecting upon our behavior and acknowledging the fact that in many cases, we are closer today to some irrational ancestor, than to a well-balanced being capable of facing reality with utmost consciousness.

However, further specification was sought and thus Anthropology tells us that closer to us, only some fifty thousand years ago, stands *Sapiens sapiens*, that is, the *Homo* who knows he knows; the human being of today, in other words, us. But this maximum knowledge of our species grows dim when we consider the performance of men and women, our contradictions and violence, our ravings that seem to be guiding us to some sort of collective suicide, our pettiness that distance us from those whom with must live with and build an inhabitable world.

The knowledge which has allowed us to dominate nature to such an extent that we have almost eradicated age-old diseases, to be aware of things so small that it is hard to imagine they exist, or something so large that it exceeds all efforts to understand it, this same knowledge has not served to eradicate the poverty and starvation of our own brothers and sisters. Moreover, at times it seems that more intelligence is dedicated to perfecting the structure that creates poverty on the one hand and superabundance on the other, than to overcoming this scourge.

There is no doubt that humans are the most intelligent beings on Earth and that we are capable of noble and heroic acts. Despite our erratic and even unhealthy behavior, we are even dying for something practically undefinable that we call love.

As biological beings, we have bodies that strive to find food and water, and to ensure those two or three minutes of oxygen essential to the continuity of life. However, together with this indisputable material reality, we as human beings perceive a deep dimension in our lives that has to do with the ability to see beyond the surface of things, to conceive reality as a space greater than mere visual or tactile appearance. Also, to know that the life that beats inside is more than the body that is exposed to the weather or modestly covered. The poet Walt Whitman said it with characteristic beauty:

> ...and am not contain'd
> between my hat and my boots.
>
> (From Walt Whitman, *Song of Myself*)

In the Beginning, Those Words

IN THE BEGINNING, GOD was busy creating things which He gave to Adam to name. At first they were mostly animals, and easy to define. But then came more complex objects, and as time passed, the horizon expanded and more words needed to be found. It wasn't an easy task.

Then came Eve, who also had to take up this essential task of naming objects. As their eyes observed the unfolding surroundings, their skin soaked up sensations through their pores, and their ears were struck with all kinds of sounds.

And so it was that they felt the hardness of an object and called it *stone*, from which sprang the words *stony, sandstone* and *stoning*. They perceived the vastness of their surroundings and called it *land*, setting the base to the much later use of *landscape, landing* and *landmark*.

Adam must have called the color of the celestial vault *blue*, and Eve was sensitive to the lightness and puffiness of those traveling spots which seemed so delicate to her and she called them by a word so soft that it seems to float: *cloud*. One night they startled awake, looked at each other and said together: *tremor, earthquake*. That night they knew and named fear and anguish, and they no longer slept.

But something unsettled them, something for which they could not find the right word. An inexplicable vibration asked to be named. *Eve was so pretty when he saw her exploring among the stones and studying the fronds of a fern*, thought Adam; *Adam looked so vigorous when he climbed up high to reach the ripest fruit,* mused Eve. How could you put into words these intimate feelings; what sound could reflect them? It was strange and it was new. To be sure, it was one of the hard words, those that did not come at once.

We do not know who first uttered these words, whether it was Eve or Adam. But from the innermost depths, one of them said for the first time: *I like you.* And the other one answered: *It will be so good.*

(Genesis 2:19–20)

Getting One's Bearings in the World

THE NEEDLES OF OUR current day compasses point north and south in the same direction as our maps place north on top and south in the bottom. However, it hasn't always been this way. One of the words we still use today reveals this: to "orientate oneself" means to find the orient.

The oldest maps we know to date were "orientated," that is, they placed the orient upwards. The Assyrians did so fifteen centuries before Christ, and the Hebrews and all the peoples of that region followed this tradition. This fact should not come as a surprise, as it derives from one of the most elemental of all human experiences: waiting for the sun to rise. Thus, "orientating one's self" meant watching where the sun came up and calling that place "the front," and the opposite—sun down—"behind."

Thus, our East (*qedem*, front, in Hebrew) and West (*aharon*, behind, past) have those names in the Bible. North is called *tzafon* and means "hidden" or "concealed," probably because Israel always felt more comfortable going south toward the desert, than towards the lands of the north, which were inhabited by more powerful cultures. When they faced the east, the right hand pointed to the south. In Hebrew, south is *iamin*, which means, the right. That is why Benjamin, the name of Jacob's last son, means "son of the right" or "son of the south," which is where that tribe was located on the map of Israel.

Several things were orientated at that time. The door of the temple of Jerusalem faced east, so that the sun would enter through it very early. The Garden of Eden was located in the east (Genesis 2:8) and Jonah camped east of Nineveh. From the East will come He who will free the Israelites from the Babylonian captivity (Isaiah 41:2) and from this same East He will take them to restore their land in Judah.

Much later, the wise men who sought the newborn Jesus, would also come from the Orient.

Dry Bones

WIND MOVES SHIPS AND windmills. It billows out flags and clears the skies. It also destroys and topples trees. Wind can be friendly or fearful, a blessing or a catastrophe. In the Bible, wind is a frequently named natural element, perhaps because it is perceived as one of the most primitive experiences: does anyone remember the first time that strange and invisible force was felt?

There are several different uses for the word "wind" in the Old Testament. The Spirit of God is called *ruach*, which means "the wind of breath." This is why there are situations in which God's *ruach* blows and others, in which the wind simply blows. However, both winds come from the Creator.

The prophet Ezekiel was taken to a valley full of human bones. In the Biblical tradition, human bones transmit impurity and should not be touched. We are told that Ezekiel had to walk close by them, perhaps with a certain amount of fear or reverence. And there they were, old dry bones, remnants of forgotten beings. Since Adam had created the word "land," he could say that there were so many bones, that they covered the entire landscape. Could all those dry old bones join back together and come alive?

The prophet carried out his office and prophesied what God had told him. In a marvelous whirlwind, the bones began to come together and find each other, much like someone putting together the pieces of broken ceramic jar. Next came the tendons and the flesh; until the skin covered all into place. They had everything but the wind, that force which fills the sails and cools the evening heat. And this wind only comes from God.

One more word from the prophet was enough, and from the four winds came the wind. For it is the Spirit of God that vivifies and amalgamates life, by joining the parts together so that they cease to be separate pieces placed next to each other, to become a body. The presence of the Spirit, that mysterious wind, completed what was lacking. And they became a vast army.

(Ezekiel 37:1–14)

Names

IN ANCIENT TIMES, THERE was a passion for seeing beauty in certain animals and expressing it in names: Rachel means sheep. Deborah means bee. Jonah is a man's name, but in its original Hebrew, *yonah* meant "dove."

In the Bible, Susana (*shoshanah*) is the word that names a lily and is related to the number six, for the petals of the lilies. Curiously, Azucena also derives from the same Semitic word, but reached us through the Arabs who lived in Spain. Note the coincidence in the sound of the consonants of the two names; from the same root, the name took different routes to arrive in different forms to the same Spanish language.

The name Leila holds the mystery of the night (*laila* means "night" in Hebrew). Esther is the name of the Persian goddess Ishtar. In Persian, *estara* means "star" and passed almost unchanged into English.

The book of Ruth (a name which means "friend, friendship") introduces us to Naomi, whose meaning in Hebrew is "sweet" or "graceful one," while Mara (alas!) means bitter, bitterness.

David means "beloved." Another great monarch Salomon, bears in his name the idea of a pacifier (in Hebrew it is *shelomó*, very close to the word *shalom*—peace).

Names that include the syllable *el* are a whole other chapter. They are called theophories, that is, God is included in them. Daniel means "God is my judge," understood as "only God can judge me" (*dan* is "judge" in Hebrew). Manuel (also Emmanuel) means

"God is with us." Raphael means "God is my physician." Gabriel and Gabriella mean "man (or woman) of God" (*geber, geberet* are man and woman in Hebrew). Finally, "my mountain, fortress, rock, is God" is expressed by Ariel (*ar* is "mount" in Hebrew).

Delilah (same in Hebrew *delilah*) means "weak," "languishing," which does not do justice to her courage and ingenuity in deceiving Samson (Hebrew *shimshon*), also the name of a Canaanite deity. According to his name, Samson believed himself to be practically a god, but he was actually so weak that he lost his power when his hair was cut.

The Female Disciples

A DISCIPLE IS A person who adheres to a doctrine under the guidance of a master. The prophets had disciples, as did the Pharisees and John the Baptist. As we know, Jesus had disciples.

Usually, we consider that Jesus had twelve disciples. Their names are given in several texts, with a few variations: in Matthew 10:1–4 they coincide, with some minor discrepancies, with the lists in the other Gospels and Acts 1:13, where Mathias is chosen to replace Judas Iscariot after his death. It is true that Jesus gave special attention to a group of twelve disciples in order to give them special training (Matthew 11:1), but it is also true that a crowd followed Him on the road and many of them were also considered disciples.

Matthew 27:55 mentions that many women were at the foot of the cross, as that they had followed Him from Galilee. In two places, Luke (vv. 23:27 and 49) confirms this version of a group of women who followed Jesus on his journeys. Without forcing the meaning of the text, we have every right to consider this large group as disciples of Jesus. If we consider woman's secondary place in those times, we can discern how brave and transgressing it must have been for women to leave their homes alone and follow their master on the road. At one time, Jesus deemed it necessary to extend the preaching and designated seventy disciples, in pairs, to prepare the way for Him in every town (Luke 10:1–17). We do not know if there were women among them, but there is nothing said against it.

Acts 6:1–2 says that the number of disciples had grown until it had become a multitude. This is because in that book the word disciple is synonymous with Christian and, consequently, each new believer was considered a disciple. We already have the names of Sapphira and the "disciple" Dorcas (Acts 9:36). Acts 9:19 mentions that there were disciples in Damascus, quite a distance from the region where Jesus acted during his life.

What may be cause for surprise or doubt to us, was not so for the first Christians. For them, it was common for women to be part of the leadership of the emerging Church.

Year One

It was the year 1269 in the Roman calendar. This calendar counted the years from the foundation of Rome, and governed all documents in the western world. Dionysius Exiguus,—or "Dennis the Small," because he was short in stature—wished to replace this method for counting years with a new calendar beginning with the Christian era. To do this, it was necessary to establish the year in which Jesus had been born, something that until then no one had thought of determining. Dionysius was a monk and well versed in the science of his time. He mastered mathematics and history, and was an expert in astronomy. He fulfilled every condition for carrying out this task.

With the means available at the time, he calculated dates, estimated stellar data and pored over books in the library. After much investigation, he sentenced the sought-after date, the year in which the Lord had been born. At that time, he concluded that they were living in the year 527 after the birth of Christ. However, even those who know a lot, make mistakes, and Dionysius Exiguus was no exception. Pope Hormisdas—who had commissioned the task—blessed the new date, and we have been dragging the error in our calendar ever since.

Much later it was possible to ascertain that Herod the Great died in the year 4 before Christ. Since the Gospels tell that Jesus was born in the days of Herod, it is obvious that his birth had to have taken place one or two years before the ruler's death, that is, in our current year 5 or 6 before Christ.

Dionysius also confirmed, through his doubtful scientific research, that the birth of Jesus had taken place on December 25th, a date which coincided with the *Natalis Solis Invicti*, a Roman pagan celebration for the Birthday of the Unconquered Sun. In the northern hemisphere, this is the date of the spring solstice, when the days begin to lengthen. Therefore, it celebrated the victory of the sun over the darkness which until then had taken minutes away from the light every day.

The Crying Child

SHE PREPARED THE BASKET with watery eyes, and a trembling in her stomach that she could not control. It all seemed so absurd, so terrible, but there was no longer an alternative. A child that cries reveals its presence and the punishment is death. The instructions were clear and ruthless: children are our enemies and a threat to our future; they must be cast into the river to ensure our peace and prosperity, proclaimed the decree. Anguished, in the middle of the night, she stealthily sought a place in which to leave him. There were shame and bitterness in her steps. She kissed him. She softly murmured a sweet song in his ear. She caressed the bright brown cheeks with her hand and she covered the basket so that she would no longer see him.

The hours pass, the afternoon arrives and the child cries. He is the only baby who is said to cry in the entire Bible. By crying, the child claims what he wants to say: *I'm hungry; I'm cold; I want to live; I'm here*. There are no tears or language yet, but the message is clear. He stirs, he moves and he waits in vain for the well-known scent and hand of his mother.

A young woman approaches and opens the basket. Her eyes moisten and her stomach trembles because she understands what is happening. She thinks in horror: *He is a child of the Hebrews*. She knows of the hard fate that awaits him. He is the child of slaves, of those weaklings, of the foreigners who shape the clay. She works in the palace and knows the law and her duty as an Egyptian woman.

She knows of discipline, of loyalty to the king, of the punishment for traitors, of the dagger or cell that awaits those who disobey.

The child cries more loudly now and his crying has more power than the orders of the most powerful man on Earth. The young woman makes a decision: she lifts the baby into her arms, warms him against her breast and takes him to the Pharaoh's daughter. That day he was given the name Moses.

(Exodus 2:1–10)

Charles Darwin, God and Primates

THOSE WHO CONSIDER CHARLES Darwin and his theory of evolution to be enemies of the Christian faith, not only betray their ignorance, but show that they have not read his books nor bothered to understand his thinking. There is nothing better than to read a few paragraphs from his famous works *The Origin of Species* and *The Descent of Man*:

> There is grandeur in this view of life, with its several powers, having been originally breathed by the Creator into a few forms or into one; and that, whilst this planet has gone circling on according to the fixed law of gravity, from so simple a beginning endless forms most beautiful and most wonderful have been, and are being evolved. (On the Origin of Species)

> To believe that man was aboriginally civilized and then suffered utter degradation in so many regions, is to take a pitiably low view of human nature. It is apparently a truer and more cheerful view that progress has been much more general than retrogression; that man has risen, though by slow and interrupted steps, from a lowly condition to the highest standard as yet attained by him in knowledge, morals and religion. (The Descent of Man)

And in his books Darwin does not hesitate to talk about

> "...the laws impressed on matter by the Creator..." (O of S)

Two more paragraphs from Charles Darwin for us to think about:

> *The question is of course wholly distinct from that higher one, whether there exists a Creator and Ruler of the Universe; and this has been answered in the affirmative by some of the highest intellects that have ever existed.* (O of S)

And this one:

> *Many existing superstitions are the remnants of former false religious beliefs. The highest form of religion—the grand idea of God hating sin and loving righteousness—was unknown during primeval times.* (O of S)

In some other paragraph of his book, he writes between the lines that fully aware of human behavior in his time—for Darwin rejected and was hurt by slavery, violence and war—he was happier harking back to those ancestors that, hanging freely from trees, enjoyed the gifts of the Creator.

The Elamite at Pentecost

For Alicia Casas

ON THAT DAY HE understood the value and the drama of words. They have flavor when we know them, but are an unsurmountable barrier when they are strange to us. That is why the growing noise and their modulations made them seem drunk; at times, he also thought they were intoxicated until, among the multitude of sounds, he heard one that was familiar. From the vortex of confusing voices, a string of words arose which he was able to identify. He heard Elamite.

He had arrived from Elam the previous afternoon and did not expect to hear his language in Jerusalem. Like all the Jews of his country, he spoke and communicated in Aramaic, the common tongue of the entire region. But he proudly kept to himself the articulation of Elamite, the tongue of his ancestors. A language uncontaminated by Hindu or Semitic words, similar to Sumerian, the first tongue human beings ever put into writing. Elamite was of the lineage of the first traces of letters ever written in the mud to represent a sound. With its elder Sumerian brothers, they had invented history, recorded memory, and filled libraries.

His blood still rankled against the vile warrior Alexander the Great, who mutilated the Elamite language and replaced it with the crude Greek symbols. Since then, the treasure of the words of his land had gradually been relegated to the heart, to the intimacy of home, and, without meaning to, each generation allowed their words to be defeated and buried by the passage of time.

For this reason he was surprised to hear Elamite amid the murmur. But it grew clearer and stronger. There was a strong wind in the room and a clamor, but neither the wind nor the clamor bothered him. In the midst of the emotion that engulfed him, he had a vision of graves opening up and springing out words that inaugurated names; he felt that which only happens in dreams and consists of hearing new words, but feeling that we have known them forever. It was as though the words knew him. What they were saying to him came from the origins of time and projected strongly into the future.

Then he saw the brightness descend upon them.

(Acts 2:1–13)

More Names

IN THE OLD TESTAMENT, Aaron's and Moses' sister was called Miriam. The origin of this name is unknown, although it probably derives from an Egyptian word. When it was translated into Greek, it became Mary, and so it appears by mistake in many Bibles in Exodus 15:20 and other passages that mention her. Miriam was a woman of character, the first to be called a prophetess, and leader of the women who sang and danced after crossing the Red Sea. Perhaps it was because of her strength and bravery that only she was punished when she challenged Moses for his sexual misconduct (Numbers 12). She made the accusation together with her brother Aaron, but nothing is said about his punishment.

Joseph (*yosef* in Hebrew) means "he who adds" (*yasaf* is "to add" in Hebrew). Height, soft curves and sharp profile embodied the name Tamara, which is feminine and means palm tree. With Mark, which is a Latin name, we have two alternatives: it may derive from the word for hammer, in the sense of strength and power, but it also may come from Mars, the god who was the son of Jupiter and Juno, who was devoted to war and gave strength to the fighters. It is probable that both meanings are connected to this name. Andrew is a Greek word that means "male," and was also related to bravery and virility.

There are names that sparkle: Sarah in Hebrew means "princess." Leah probably means "wild cow," which in that time was a compliment that all women wished to hear, and accepted with modesty. We are told that her eyes were tender and pleasant

(Genesis 29:16), but her charm was not enough to seduce Jacob, who fell in love with her sister Rachel, for such is the way of the heart, a story that we will look into later on.

From the theophoric name Nathanael come our Nathan and Natalie. It means "gift of God" (*natan* in Hebrew is a word related to giving and the suffix *el* means "God").

Joshua (*yehoshua*) means "the savior." He succeeded Moses and led the people of Israel when they reached the Promised Land, a land of salvation and abundance for those who came from slavery and the desert. From the aridity of the desert they went to a land flowing with milk and honey, where the sickle and the plough could do their work. Many centuries later, a man called Joshua—we know him by the Greek form: Jesus—would also cross a border and invite others to cross it with him.

Christopher Columbus and the Bible

THE BIBLE MUST BE read and studied, and it has to be done correctly. For it can be read in such a way that it leads to error, as in the case of Christopher Columbus, although in this case, the mistake led to a happy ending.

Towards the end of the 15th century, the list of books that make up the Bible had not yet been defined. They varied according to the different Christian traditions. If we compare our current Bible with the one used at that time—the Latin Vulgate Bible that Western Christianity read during the Middle Ages and that Catholicism used until well into the 20th century—it had about fifteen more books. Among these was the one called the Second Book of Esdras (2 Esdras), a work also known as the Apocalypse of Esdras or the Book of the Prophet Esdras. It was part of the Old Testament; it was read as such and no one dared to question its standing as Sacred Scripture.

Christopher Columbus was convinced that the Earth was round and that if he set out westward he would reach the east. But not knowing the distance worried him, and this factor was crucial for calculating the time the voyage would take and the realistic possibilities of reaching the goal. As a true believer, he resorted to the Bible and in it he scrutinized the Second Book of Esdras, whose content reviews and enlarges the seven days of creation. Columbus used 6:42 as the basis for calculating the distance between the coast of the Kingdom of Portugal and the extreme

Orient which was called India. In this text he found the light he was seeking. It reads like this:

> ... *on the third day you commanded the waters to be gathered together in a seventh part of the earth; but you made six parts dry and preserved them so that some of these might be sown and cultivated* ...

He reflected that if the sea only occupied one seventh of the Earth against six parts covered by firm ground, a few days of sailing westward would take him to the coast of India.

Columbus died without knowing that he had been greatly mistaken. He had read the Biblical text literally, not realizing that it was symbolic, that it was not a geography manual, for only one fourth of the earth's surface consists of firm ground. However, fate took pity on the admiral. An unknown continent between Europe and the Indies allowed him to rest from his hectic voyages convinced of his sagacity in interpreting Scripture.

(From Christopher Columbus, *Diary of the Third Voyage*)

A Love Story
Jacob and Rachel

DARKNESS AND DRINK HAD their effect and, after spending the first night with the woman he thought he had chosen, he woke up in the morning to realize it was someone else. He had worked seven years to get Rachel, but it was Leah who was in his bedsheets.

He wasted no time to complain, as his father-in-law gave him all kinds of excuses to justify what he had done. He proposed giving him Rachel after one week if he agreed to work another seven years as payment for her. Thus, the father made sure of placing his elder daughter Leah and wagered that Jacob—whom he knew was seduced by the body of his other daughter—would not hesitate to agree. After all, thought Jacob, seven years had been like a few days to him in order to get Rachel. Another sever years would not be burdensome, especially if she was delivered in advance and he could now enjoy being with the woman he loved. In the eyes of love, fourteen years of labor did not seem like a long time.

It had all started at the well. Rachel arrived leading her sheep and, when Jacob first saw her, he kissed her, he wept and he raised his voice because he knew that he had found the woman for whom he had been waiting for. She stood out for her bronzed face and her slender figure; he had never perceived in another woman that special fragrance that her body exhaled at the end of a long day in the hills with her flock of sheep. A fragrance that was true to her, for Rachel means sheep—she was that beautiful. Rachel was different from the others, and Jacob felt a strange vibration when he walked passed her tent or when he saw her fading into the distance in the desert, leading her sheep. "It's worth leaving everything for a woman like that," thought Jacob.

In the long run, his father-in-law's trick meant that Jacob received four women: Leah and Rachel as wives as well as Bilhah and Zilpah, the two slaves that accompanied them. Faithful to his heart, Jacob always loved Rachel more than Leah and the slaves, which gave rise to jealousy and conflicts among them, and when doing business too. For example, at one point Rachel received a few mandrakes from Leah, to allow Jacob to sleep with her, with such good fortune for Leah that that night she conceived another son when she thought she was sterile and would not give birth again.

Between the four women, they gave Jacob twelve sons and one daughter; Dinah the curious.

(Genesis 29–30)

Albert Schweitzer or Reverence for Life

HE WAS BORN WHERE Germany and France meet, but he was French. As a young man he challenged thought with his new ideas about the life of Jesus and the ethical consequences of his preaching. He realized that being a Christian was not worth much if the love for one's neighbor proclaimed in the Bible did not translate into a radical defense of life in all of its forms, especially, protecting human dignity.

He was a renowned theologian when at thirty years of age he decided to study medicine and surgery in order to devote his life to helping the poorest and most abused community of his time. Around 1913 he moved to Lambaréné, present-day Gabon, a nation on the African Atlantic. There he founded a hospital and cared for thousands of persons. Most of those who sought help suffered from leprosy and the "sleeping disease," a deadly illness of that region. Albert treated them with affection, respected them and made them feel that they were important for just having been born. He not only cured with medicine, but with the profound conviction that each person is unique and precious in the eyes of God.

But being a doctor did not make him give up his other two passions. He was a musician and a talented organ player. He worked out a style for performing Bach's pieces that is used and appreciated to this day. And he did not stop writing as well. His thoughts on philosophy and theology can be summarized by the title of one of his works: *Reverence for Life*. Schweitzer maintained that, from the tiny beetle to the imposing elephant, everyone was here with a purpose and their lives should be protected and revered. There could be no argument for destroying that which was sacred and imprinted on every being. If the life of a coleopteran was sacred, how could the life of each man and woman who inhabit this earth fail to be so?

Like all his generation, he experienced the tragedy of the two great world wars. He was opposed to them and devoted part of his life to proclaiming that armaments and the use of nuclear energy as a weapon of war were detestable and consumed the financial resources that should be applied to the development and wellbeing of the world's population. Without wars and without weapons, there would be enough money for humanity to no longer suffer hunger, ignorance and violence. They did not listen to him, and we still continue to live with these scourges among us.

That he received the Nobel Peace Prize and that his nephew was Jean-Paul Sartre, simply add a few anecdotal facts to his life.

Beethoven and the Ninth Symphony

Two centuries earlier, Martin Luther had intuited that God was not reached by works and good intentions. The corollary of his thought was that in order to find Him it was necessary to put faith into play, because mere reason alone would not reveal His secrets. In the late 18th century, the poet Schiller suffered for that truth and composed his *Ode to Liberty* which was censored to read "Ode to Joy."

His contemporary, Emmanuel Kant, gave form to this feeling and established through his implacable reasoning, that no matter how much we investigate the subject and however much science abounds in discoveries, God will not be reached this way. Perhaps Kant did not mean for things to be this way, but the great majority of his contemporaries who thrived on intuition and feelings, this meant that God was far from life, from relationships between persons and, especially, far from each other´s heart.

All these vectors led to one place and one person. That person was Ludwig van Beethoven, who, despite fierce deafness, composed one of the most celebrated musical works of our culture: his Ninth Symphony.

There are poets who feel constricted by syntax and chained by words, and they dream of breaking that structure. They seek to reduce words to their sounds. They long for the music of the syllables, rather than the objectivity of the words, and wish to emulate the musicians by nullifying meaning in their verses. Beethoven was driven down the opposite path. Dissatisfied with the sounds and scales he mastered as few could, tired of not being able to express what he felt, he did what no one had imagined, what only someone desperate could do: he put words to his symphony.

Now comes what we really want to convey, the justification of these lines. The world in which Beethoven lived was becoming distressed by the lack of divinity. God was no longer in things, God could no longer be found in lengthy pilgrimages to sanctuaries, and miraculous appearances were not to be trusted. It became known that a flower, however beautiful, no longer revealed the Creator. Also that human life was no guarantee of his existence. Even if for ages institutions—the Church, philosophy, reason—had ensured contact with God and the peace of His blessing, now everything was in the hands of each person. God is only found through faith, and faith is an act of will, an action that we have to perform, a human initiative subject to our ups and downs and our different moods. Sometimes we cling to it and at other times it escapes us.

Not surprisingly, Beethoven modified Schiller's poem and rewrote it to his own taste. It is almost a paraphrase, a way of resorting to him without being tied by his words. What he could not say with music he said with borrowed words:

> *Brothers, beyond the stars*
> *must a loving Father dwell. . ..*
> *World, do you sense your creator?*
> *Seek him then beyond the stars.*

There are no longer certainties nor tutors. The God who can no longer be reached by reason has not abandoned humanity. He is still there and can be felt when we contemplate the immensity of the stars.

Psalm 8

He walked toward the rock where every night he sat to rest. It was near his house and its shape allowed him to lie down and see the sky. His wife was feeding the baby, born four weeks before; the other children already slept. He removed his sandals, because he liked to feel the earth itself beneath his feet. He felt that in this way his feet connected him to what was below the earth and his eyes to what was above the earth.

Then she arrived. Now the baby also slept. She sat beside him, on the same rock, and, as she did every night, she held his hand.

He thought about her hands, when she spun with her fingers and made those blankets to warm them in winter. She thought about the baby falling asleep at her breast, about that pink mouth that joined them and through which flowed milk and love.

A movement, a noise, reminded them that the sheep and the ox also slept in the yard, and that tomorrow would be a long work day. Suddenly they saw a falling star. They saw them almost every night and they loved to think about what a star might be like, where it might fall, and if someone might pick it up. He asked her, "Do you think a star will ever fall near us so we can pick it up and show it to the children? She answered, "I don't know." And they remained silent for a long time. It was one of those nights with a small moon, a thinning bow, almost gone, and she wondered about that opening and closing of the moon, so inexplicable and so beautiful.

They gazed at the sky. They measured distances by stades; they never knew what a light year was. Neither did they know what a star was or why they disappeared by day, but they knew that the town that lived behind the hills, their friends, who talked to the moon and awaited a reply, would never receive one. The moon was there to be admired, not to be spoken to. They did not know about the atom nor did they imagine a galaxy; for them the earth did not extend much beyond the circle of the horizon, that strange line that could never be reached.

They were almost asleep on top of the rock and beneath the sky. They liked that moment because it was when they gathered words and played with them. They did not know how they did that either, because they were words that came to them from inside. She told him, "Before going home to sleep, let's say those words we began to build and let's add others, something about children." He said, "Yes, and something about fingers." And they began saying them together, very softly, so as not to wake anyone:

O Lord, our Lord, how majestic is your name in all the earth...

And they continued weaving words until they went to sleep.

The Apostle Julia

In the libraries of Michigan and Dublin dwell the treasures that Sir Alfred Chester Beatty collected throughout his life. Among the works of art and rare pieces, there is also a collection of Islamic, Persian and Chinese texts, including several papyri from the Old and New Testaments.

Only one of the three New Testament papyri interests us at this time, the so-called P 46, which contains the Epistles of Paul. And from this papyrus, verse 7 of chapter 16 of the Epistle to the Romans. There, in the papyrus, the Apostle Paul says: "...greet Andronicus and Julia, my kinsfolk and my fellow prisoners; they are of note among the apostles...." Later he mentions that they were both Christians before he was. There is no room for doubt: Julia was an apostle and perhaps the wife of Andronicus.

This mention of the Apostle Julia also appears in the Bible called the Vetus Latina (the "old" Latin, prior to the Vulgate which was published in the year 382 replacing it) and in the translation of the Bible to the Coptic language, which is late Egyptian. The oldest Bibles mention "Julia." However, this name is replaced by the name Junias—a word in masculine form—in all Bible versions beginning in the 5th century. And that is how it has been reproduced until it reached our modern bibles.

It is difficult to hide the truth and, although a long time may go by, that which is authentic rises to the surface. There are two arguments in favor of Julia, each different and each indisputable. The first is that the studies of all ancient Greek and Latin literature, of all the literary texts, of their theater and lyrics, of their history and philosophy, have not found a single instance of the name Junias. Junias, as a name, does not exist.

The second argument involves a sage. In the late 4th century, John Chrysostom, the greatest preacher and theologian of his day, bishop and patriarch of Constantinople, when preaching on Romans 16:7 said, "How great was the devotion of this woman that she should be deemed worthy of being called an apostle!"

John Chrysostom read Paul's Epistles in their original version, before they were adulterated.

(From St. John Chrysostom,
Homily on the Epistle to the Romans)

Casiodoro de Reina, Bible Translator

CASIODORO DE REINA WAS a monk from Seville who, like so many others of his generation, felt the contradiction between the faith that sustained his life and the teachings of the Church. He became convinced that what the Church needed was to know the Bible better and that the more it was read and studied, the better off the people and the world would be.

That was when he had a very daring dream: to translate and publish the entire Bible into the Spanish language. Until then no one had done so and there were only fragmentary versions, a few individual books and a translation of the Old Testament by the Jews of Spain. In addition, none of these writings were accessible to the people.

Casiodoro had powerful tools, since his erudition included knowledge of the Biblical languages (Hebrew, Aramaic and Greek) and Latin, a language that was very useful at that time. Even more essential and to the point, he had the firm conviction that this undertaking was necessary in order for the Gospel to spread and escape from the prison in which it was chained.

He was a monk who converted to Protestantism, who was condemned as a heretic and fled before the Inquisition would burn him at the stake. Together with him, the community of monks from the convent of San Isidro del Campo left the city at night and headed for Geneva. On April 26, 1562 a figure representing him went up in flames in Seville (it was called "burning in effigy");

but others were not as lucky and were murdered in person. Casiodoro was able to reach Frankfurt, but his life was still in danger. King Philip II put a price on his head and infiltrated the circles he frequented with spies, once again forcing him to leave. He was in London, Strasbourg, Ambers and other cities. On his journeys he carried the translation of the Bible, which grew at a fast pace.

While he translated, he also accomplished other tasks. He published Bible commentaries, wrote a catechism and translated several works into Spanish. In 1567 he wrote and published in Heidelberg the first book against the Inquisition and signed it with the pseudonym Reginaldus Gonsalvius Montanus.

But Casiodoro's goal was to publish the Bible and he worked endlessly toward that end. In 1567 the translation was ready and he hired one of the best publishers of the day, but he died before beginning the work. This delayed publication, forcing him to find another publisher and more money. Finally, on June 24, 1569, from a printing house in Basel, the Book of the Bear came to light, thus called because of the engraving of a bear on the cover. Two thousand six hundred copies were printed. Only a few books from that first edition survived; first the Inquisition—which condemned it to bonfire and destroyed hundreds—and then the natural passing of time decimated the rest of the copies. Today a few remain scattered across Europe and in Buenos Aires.

After publishing his translation of the Bible, he lived in the city of Ambers, in present-day Belgium, until the Spaniards conquered it and he was once again forced to flee. He returned to Frankfurt, where he earned his living selling cloth and tapestries. During his stay in London he had been ordained as pastor in the Anglican Church, and in that city he found a Spanish-speaking congregation who received him as such.

Casiodoro was born in Seville in 1520 and died in Frankfurt in 1594. He left us a translation of the Bible that endures—with adaptations—in our churches to this day.

The Bible of the Bear

When the phrase "In a village of La Mancha whose name I do not wish to recall. . ." was not yet familiar to anyone because many years were still to pass before it was written, the first complete translation of the Bible into Spanish appeared in a print shop in Basel.

Casiodoro de Reina had worked for years to give Spanish-speaking believers a Bible text they could read in their own language. Until its publication in 1569, the Bible could only be read in Latin (the translation known as the Vulgate), a language most common folk didn't speak, and even if they did, they didn't have access to any copies.

The editor was called Samuel Biener (his surname means "beekeeper" in German) and in the editorial seal that illustrated the cover he used the figure of a bear towering over a tree, trying to reach a container full of honeycombs. When he published the Bible, he added on the seal, at the foot of the tree, an open book with Hebrew letters spelling YHWH, the name of God in that tongue, which in the Bible text appears as Jehovah. In addition, he placed the following text at the foot in Hebrew and Spanish: "The word of our God remains forever," taken from Isaiah 40:8.

Because of this seal on the cover, it is known as "The Bible of the Bear." This translation, with the small corrections made by Cipriano de Valera, is the one that Evangelical people still recognize today as the translation that is most widespread and commonly used in the churches.

There are some characteristics that make this translation a masterpiece. Protestantism insisted in returning to God's word, and to do so, it encouraged translations into modern languages that would allow its wide distribution among people.

Casiodoro decided to translate the Bible from Hebrew, Aramaic and Greek, the original languages of the Bible text. He avoided translating it from Latin, which would have been simpler but did not ensure maximum fidelity to the message. If, as we know, all translation implies some distance from the original text, how much more distance would there be in a translation from a translation?

Casiodoro's version includes the so-called apocryphal books in its edition. In this it follows the books found in the Vulgate Bible, since at that time the Protestants had still not established their position on whether or not they should remain as Bible text or be considered works of spiritual edification and useful to the faith but not part of the Sacred Scriptures. At the Council of Trent, held between 1545 and 1563, the Catholic Church had just decreed that several of these books would remain in their Bibles, but in the Protestant world the excision of these works took place gradually during the 17th century.

Finally, the Spanish style that Casiodoro gave to his translation is worthy of note. At a time when the Golden Age of Spanish literature was just beginning, this Bible is a monument to the beauty and plasticity of the Spanish language. He not only transferred a message requiring delicate translation, but he did so with uncommon grace and accuracy.

The Old Testament is written in Semitic languages with which there are no linguistic contacts and, therefore, it is often expressed in phrases and words that are difficult to transpose to our language; the Greek of the New Testament also posed challenges, especially because of its different syntactical structure and the complexity of the message in some of the books. Casiodoro used other previous translations, but improved them by study, erudition and sensitivity until he achieved a text of the highest quality.

The Bible of the Bear

When there were still no models of Spanish prose and poetry to open stylistic paths, Casiodoro opened the way for others to continue elevating the language.

To Casiodoro, the Word must have tasted like the best wild honey.

The Bible of the Jar, the Reina-Valera

In 1602, the first revision of the translation by Casiodoro de Reina was published in Amsterdam. The reviser was Cipriano de Valera, and the Bible would be known first as the Bible of the Jar and, much later, to honor those who worked on it, as the Reina-Valera Bible.

It was called "of the Jar" because the seal on its cover shows a tree and two persons, one of which is pouring water onto the earth from a jar, as if watering a newly planted tree. Above them, illuminating the scene, are the Hebrew letters for God's name, YHWH.

The Bible of the Jar does not contain many differences from Casiodoro's text, but there are differences of form and accessory items. Cipriano modified almost all the marginal references from the first edition and reduced some of the introductions and summaries with which the books and chapters began, but added them to the Book of Revelation, which had none. Another important change was the order of the books. In the Bible of the Bear, the apocryphal books are interspersed with the rest of the books of the Old Testament, while Cipriano considered that it was better to group them and place them at the end, before the New Testament.

Cipriano had belonged to the group of monks from the convent of San Isidro del Campo in Seville who had fled to Geneva in 1557 to escape from the bonfire of the Inquisition. The leader of the group was Casiodoro de Reina and they fled together, but then their lives took separate paths: Casiodoro remained an

The Bible of the Jar, the Reina-Valera

independent Protestant, while Cipriano embraced the doctrines of John Calvin. Their dwelling places were also different. Cipriano settled down in England, where he became a distinguished professor at Oxford and Cambridge, while Casiodoro went from city to city throughout Europe, always in search of a place in which to settle down.

Cipriano took on the revision of the Bible for several reasons. In his prologue he said that it was because the 2,600 copies of the Bible of the Bear had been bought up. However, we know that there were other less practical reasons. Cipriano's Calvinist emphasis made him prefer a text with different information and notes, where the apocryphal books were presented as less connected to the rest of the Old Testament. In practice, the Bible of the Jar differs from the Bible of the Bear much more in its notes and summaries than in the Bible text.

Finally, there was one more reason: there was a certain enmity between them. Cipriano was suspicious of Casiodoro's independent ideas, and the latter did not feel comfortable with the disciples of Calvin. Perhaps in order not to hurt him, Cipriano waited until Casiodoro's death—which took place in 1594—to revise and publish the translation in 1602. The cover bears only his name, although the prologue inside mentions that the text is a revision of Casiodoro's work. This resulted in the Reina-Valera being known as the Bible of Cipriano de Valera for the next three centuries. It was not until the late 19th century that Reina's name would be included in the current editions.

Water is poured from the jar on the cover for the tree to grow and become strong. We do not know if that seal was intentional, but it is a good representation of the Bible of Reina and Valera.

End of the Reformation in Seville, Spain

MARCELINO MENÉNDEZ Y PELAYO, a Spanish scholar of the late 19th century, tells of the end of Protestant thinking in Seville. Here are some fragments from his work:

> "A diabolical children's teacher named Fernando de San Juan, rector of the College of Doctrine, contributed not a little to the spread of the sect. Poor children and poor women! There were María Bohorques, learned in the Latin tongue; her sister Doña Juana; Doña Francisca Chaves; Doña Isabel de Baena, whose house was 'the temple of the new light.'"

Later he says:

> "According to one manuscript report that I own, the congregation was given away by a woman. . ., the prisons filled with people, more than 800 persons. The Holy Office rapidly heard all these cases."

> "The *auto de fe* was scheduled for September 24, 1559. Don Juan Ponce de León retracted but later recanted and returned to his old errors. The same was true of the preacher Juan González who defended himself with texts from the Scriptures."

> "The women were stubborn and extremely tenacious, especially Doña María Bohorques, even though she was very young, no more than twenty-one years old.

Under torture she gave up her sister; but she did not stop defending her heresies by one point, and resisted the preaching of the Dominicans and Jesuits who admonished her in prison. They all felt pity for her youth and misused discretion; but she continued in her syllogisms and bad theologies. . .."

The story continues:

"The most dissipated was Julianillo Hernández, who died as he had lived. He went to his execution with a gag and he himself placed the bundles of wood on his head... With him died Doña Francisca de Chaves, a nun from Santa Isabel, who called the inquisitors *generation of vipers*; Ana de Ribera, a widow; Juan Sastre, a layman from San Isidro; Francisca Ruiz, wife of the bailiff; María Gómez, widow of the apothecary of Lepe; Leonor Núñez, wife of a doctor from Seville, and her three daughters Elvira, Teresa and Lucía."

"Juan González walked to the auto with a gag; when it was removed he recited Psalm 106 with a firm voice: *Praise the Lord, invoke his name...* He was burned alive."

"Doña María de Virués; Doña María Coronel; Doña María Boorques. The three died garroted, though they showed few signs of repentance. At the last moment Ponce de León begged Bohorques to convert and set aside the exhortations of Friar Casiodoro de Reina; but she called him *ignorant, idiot and windbag*."

"On the other hand Doña Juana Bohorques was proclaimed to be innocent, who unfortunately had died during the torture she underwent right after giving birth."

The account concludes with:

"Here ends the story of the Reformation in Seville. The monastery of San Isidro was purified: the Catholic monks who remained there begged the Jesuits to come to their convent to indoctrinate them with good talks.

The heretical teachings of Fernando de San Juan were replaced by those of the fathers of the Company of Jesus... They began to teach grammar with a great number of students. Afterwards a course was given in humanities and another in arts and philosophy."

(From Marcelino Menéndez y Pelayo, *History of the Spanish Heretics* [1882], Book IV, Chapter 9, Section 5)

The Homunculus and Don Juan Ginés de Sepúlveda

It starts with the misconception that the other is not equal, but inferior to me. "I" seems to be superior, and the other subject, inferior, which is a way of saying that he who speaks is more important than he who remains silent. Or he who speaks loudly is greater than he who prefers courteous speech. He who shouts is greater than he who converses. The next qualification is: the other is a *homunculus*, a small, despicable man who has no value as a person.

There were few men in his generation as well read and erudite as Juan Ginés de Sepúlveda. He was a philosopher, legislator, historian and advisor to the King of Spain. But great knowledge is no guarantee of wisdom. Ginés de Sepúlveda considered American Natives to be homunculi, supporting his opinion with legalistic solidity in his *Treatise of the Just Causes of the War against the Indians*.

For this Spanish author of the times of the conquest of the Americas, the natives of these lands recently discovered by Spain, were a collection of uncivilized barbarians who needed to be subdued *for their own good*. Of course his erudition does not seem to have been enough to notice that these uncivilized beings had built pyramids superior to the Egyptian ones, as well as cities that were clean—for thousands of inhabitants—not filthy like the European ones; and that the new comers that he called "prudent, powerful and perfect" were swineherds and criminals who reached these shores from Spain and Portugal.

With great assurance and professorial confidence, Sepúlveda writes:

> "Being servants by nature, the barbarian, uncouth and inhuman men refuse to recognize domination by those who are more prudent, powerful and perfect than they; a domination that would bring them great profit, it being in addition just, by natural right, for matter to obey form, the body to obey the soul, appetite to obey reason, beasts to obey man, woman to obey her husband, children to obey their father, the imperfect to obey the perfect, the worst to obey the best, for the universal good of all things. This is the natural order that the divine and eternal law dictates be observed forever. And this doctrine has been confirmed not only by the authority of Aristotle, whom all the most excellent philosophers and theologians revere as the master of justice and the other moral virtues and as a most sagacious interpreter of nature and natural laws, but also by the words of Saint Thomas."

And in another paragraph he adds:

> "The Spaniards rule with perfect right over these barbarians of the New World and adjacent islands, who in prudence, wit, virtue and humanity are as much inferior to the Spaniards as children are to adults and women to men, there being between them as much difference as there is between savage and cruel peoples and peoples of great mercy."

(From Juan Ginés de Sepúlveda,
Treatise on the Just Causes of the War against the Indians)

The Land of the Wichis

ALDO ETCHEGOYEN TOLD ME this story which he witnessed himself. I can't recall the year, but I suppose it happened in the first decade of this century.

The *Wichi* community was gathered in the province of Formosa. It was a circle of people under some trees, some sitting on chairs, and others on the ground. They were assembled because their land and homes were being threatened by tractors and bulldozers driven by white men wanting to kick them out of their land. They had already burned some of their homes, and humiliated them in order to break down their will.

These lands have belonged to them since the beginning of time, but the white folks want to overtake them in order to expand the surrounding ranches. They had already destroyed their cemetery by bulldozing their land, demolishing their symbols and their stones. They profaned their bones and the memory of their fathers and mothers. And they are scared because they are aware of the violence white people are capable of. They say to themselves: what can you expect from people who do not respect the dead?

Men and women chat in the heat of the afternoon about the situation and express their anguish, their concern about the future of their children, the lack of hope in the heart of their youth who are forced to migrate to the cities towards an unhappy existence. They are aware that their warm dialogue with the earth which they grew up on had vanished and perhaps will never return. But now there's a new threat, and crueler at that: they are being forced to leave, to abandon their homes and their stars, the site of their sacred hills where they had learned how to live. They want them to forever forget the horizon that their forefathers had seen and watched them be born.

After a moment of silence and some words, they agree to sign a document. They state that they will not leave their land; that they will have to be killed in order to overtake their land.

Jorgelina Lozada, Woman and Pastor

IT WAS 1906 WHEN a woman was born in Bragado, at that time a square town of low houses in the Argentine *pampas*. They called her Jorgelina. Her days went by at great speed: when she was a child her family moved to Buenos Aires, to the neighborhood of Belgrano. At the age of fourteen she decided in favor of the Evangelical faith and joined the congregation of the Disciples of Christ. At the age of nineteen she graduated from the Model Institute for Women. She studied journalism and social work. In 1930 she was ordained as the first female pastor in Latin America. Eight years later she was appointed to a congregation in Villa Mitre, a small church when it begot her.

They were not easy times for a woman who wished to do work that everyone thought was only for men. Jorgelina was the first woman pastor and many were convinced that she could not do her job. Woman and pastor did not seem to go together. Time proved them wrong. Two years later, under her leadership, a temple, classrooms and a house were built; and the congregation grew.

Her itinerary continued. In 1944 she attended classes in Nashville; then she visited Canada and Switzerland. She was invited to give conferences in Puerto Rico. She could have tried to stay in any of these places. Her preparation and character would have been appreciated in all of them. But Jorgelina did not forget her origins and returned to Buenos Aires. There were many things to do in this part of the world, and she did not shy away from work.

She founded magazines, created libraries, organized women, wrote books and articles, preached, taught Sunday school, and participated in events around the world: India, Brazil and Germany.

Life does not always resemble what people understand it to be. But Jorgelina described life as a march, and hers was so. She described it as a permanent going because she understood that to stop is to begin to die or to forget the path we are in, which comes to the same thing. She also added that there was no room for delay, because those who proclaim the love of Christ as they go, know that they never walk alone because their Lord is with them every step of the way.

She was brave and obstinate; she was creative and curious; and she was a woman. Her name was Jorgelina.

Sri Lanka or Buenos Aires

PASTOR PABLO SOSA SHARED this memory. I am transcribing his words as I recall them.

As far as I remember, in 1954 the first Asian Evangelical leader visited us in Buenos Aires, Pastor Daniel T. Niles. He had been invited by the then rector of the Evangelical School of Theology, Foster Stockwell, to give the Carnahan Conferences. He arrived from his homeland, Sri Lanka, where among other important initiatives, he intended to indigenize the Gospel message, by promoting the incorporation of melodies and rhythms of the folk and popular songs of his region into our congregational songs. He was a theologian, a musician and a Methodist preacher of substance; in his blood he carried a grandfather who had been a theologian and a poet; as well as millenarian melodies. Not without effort and resistance, he carried out his task convinced that the Lord should be worshiped with the music that each people felt to be their best form of expression.

One day after lunch, Niles met with the students—at the age of twenty, I was a student, music teacher and choir director all at once—and sang for us several of his Evangelical songs with popular Asian melodies. Then he asked us: "And what do you sing at church? Folk songs?" No. We only sang hymns inherited from the churches of the United States and Europe. As "the musician" of the house, I knowingly added: "Our folk songs are not appropriate for worship." Then he asked us to sing one of our folk songs. We began with the *huayno* that we had so often sung together:

"Two little doves lamented, crying. . ., and consoled each other saying. . .." Niles listened carefully and when we finished singing, he said: "You are fools. You have these melodies and you tell me that they are not suitable for the Church?"

We listened to him respectfully, but we suspected that he could combine his folk songs with Christian singing because popular Asian songs had a spiritual substrate that was not found in our South American ones. We understood that Buddhism and the religions of India had molded popular culture and approached religious experience in a way that made them suitable for expressing the Christian faith. We thought that the collective spirituality inherent to those cultures made it possible to use their melodies and place them in the mold of our liturgy. But our folk songs are basically individual and solitary. The singer sings to be heard; the verses multiply in the hard walls of the hills and mountains, but do not allow community singing; tango is sad and full of melancholy, bearing a tragic life destiny that separates it from Christian hope. Deep within us, we felt that the raw material of our folk songs could not be used to build music suitable for church liturgy.

This is what I remember (and somewhat imagine) from Pablo Sosa's account.

We perceive that the wind blows where it may, in Sri Lank or in Buenos Aires, and Niles' words that afternoon had tempered a cord that would vibrate later on. Sosa told us that four years later, in 1958, he composed the *carnavalito* "*The Sky Sings for Joy,*" and added that he wrote it to sing at a student picnic of the School of Theology, not for church worship. It was sung there and remained dormant for fifteen slow years, until time and the church were ripe. Finally, the moment came when it could be sung on Sunday in the worship service.

The Old Testament Languages

THE OLD TESTAMENT WAS written in two languages. Most of the texts were written in Hebrew and some parts of the books of Daniel and Ezra were written in Aramaic. They are sister languages and were written with the same alphabet (called *alephat*).

Hebrew is the elder of the two languages. Its alphabet begins with the letters *aleph* and *bet*, which, after a long process, gave rise to our letters *a* and *b*. The *alephat* contains 22 letters, and whoever wishes to know them may go to Psalm 119, which is organized into 22 stanzas numbered by the letters in alphabetical order. This detail reveals that there are no numbers in Hebrew and that letters are used as numbers, again following alphabetical order. Thus, *aleph* is 1, *bet* is 2, *gimmel* is 3, *dalet* is 4, and so on.

Written Hebrew has no room for vowels, and the *alephat* only includes the 22 consonants with which words are transcribed. Readers "add" the vowels as they go along, relying on their intuition and knowledge of the words. In truth, there is almost no ambiguity in the writing, but in the 10th century of our era the rabbis worried about the correct pronunciation of words due to the lack of vowels, which could lead to misinterpretation of meaning.

Various rabbinical schools argued over the correct pronunciation of such and such words. After much investigation, they developed a system of vowels consisting of dots that were written below, above and in the middle of words, without touching them, and placed them in the Bible texts. Thus they ensured the correct pronunciation without having to change the form of the consonantal texts.

The Aramaic tongue is similar to Hebrew but has its own nuances. They were born together but, towards 300 B.C., Aramaic gradually became the international language of the entire region. People of various tongues communicated with each other in Aramaic and, little by little, it took the place of Hebrew in Israel, even within the family. Although it was never abandoned, it was relegated to the synagogue and religious services. For the synagogue assistants in Israel, it was necessary to translate the reading of the texts from Hebrew to Aramaic, so that they could be understood. This translation, which included comments and explanations, was called Targum.

Around the 1st century, Hebrew had disappeared as a commonly spoken language. Thus, Jesus spoke Aramaic although he could no doubt read and understand Hebrew, as we can see in the account of Luke 4:16–17, when he enters the synagogue and reads a text from the roll of the Prophet Isaiah, which, as usual, was written in the original Hebrew language.

It was not until the late 19th century that the Jewish community residing in Israel—then called Palestine—began to make the huge effort of reviving the old Biblical language. With the addition of modern words and some expressions that are typical of the evolution of all languages, the Hebrew language in which the Old Testament was written, is the one used today in the cities and streets of Israel.

The Koiné Greek of the New Testament

THE ENTIRE NEW TESTAMENT is written in the language of Homer, Plato and Sophocles. However, the Biblical authors used the so-called *Koiné* Greek, a word that means "common" and refers to the daily speech of the people, or popular Greek. After Alexander the Great conquered the entire world known at that time, between 334 and 323 B.C., Greek took over in the imperial territory. Expansion resulted in the classical language being modified by coming into contact with other languages and cultures, and giving birth to what is called "the common tongue." This *Koiné* Greek is not very different from the classical Greek, but has its nuances and regionalisms.

Koiné Greek was constructed on the basis of classical Greek (called "Attic"), but incorporated words from the international world in which it spread. In the case of the biblical texts, the influence of Semitic words from the Hebrew and Aramaic can be seen, as well as from the Greek in which the translation of the Old Testament known as the Septuagint was written.

Most, if not all, of the writers of the New Testament were Jews and had this translation as the Bible they read regularly in Greek; therefore, their vocabulary was influenced by this version. At the same time, they spoke common Greek like everyone else in their day. When they wrote the stories of Jesus, they did so in the language that most people could read and understand.

It is curious that there is no evidence of an attempt to preserve the words of Jesus in the Aramaic language they were pronounced in. The gospels only mention a few words in Aramaic and translate them for the Greek-speaking readers. Examples can be found in Matthew 27:46; Mark 5:41 and John 1:42.

We should reflect upon this fact. In the first place, it is obvious that from the very start, the missionary challenge was stronger than any wish to reproduce Jesus' words verbatim. The message had to be transmitted in the language that everyone understood. In the second place, the early Christians considered that the meaning of Jesus' words was more important than the language in which they were spoken. The disciples spoke to Jesus in Aramaic and that is the language in which he communicated with the crowds. However, the early Christian community—the oldest tradition—was not interested in preserving the language in which things were said, but in being faithful to the message that was being transmitted. They must have asked themselves: *What is the point of quoting Jesus word for word if very few can understand the language in which they were spoken?*

There are also nuances within the books of the New Testament. Some show a somewhat rustic Greek, like the Gospel of Mark, while others reflect a brilliant and refined language, like the Epistle to the Hebrews. Some prefer the straightforward language that we find in the Gospel of Luke and Acts, while others are given to using symbols and metaphors, like the Gospel of John and Revelation.

In no case will we find sloppy, badly written language or poor concepts. On the contrary, they all show passion for transmitting the message they had received in the best possible way.

The Septuagint and the Letter of Aristeas

AROUND THE YEAR 300 B.C., the Jews who lived outside of Israel no longer spoke Hebrew. Those who inhabited the Mediterranean coasts spoke Greek and had an increasingly hard time reading their sacred texts, which are basically our Old Testament. It was thus that the Jewish community of Alexandria, an Egyptian port in the Mediterranean, agreed to carry out the most impressive literary, intellectual and editorial work of their time: a translation of the entire Sacred Scriptures into the Greek language.

Translation, so common nowadays, was not so at that time. It required people knowledgeable in both languages, scribes to transcribe the text by hand, reviewers to reduce errors, and copyists to reproduce the new text to be sent to hundreds of synagogues. Never until that time had such an extensive and complex text been translated into another language. Never had a text considered sacred to the community of the faith, been translated so that the believers could read it in the language that was now familiar to them.

Such an undertaking deserved not only to be done, but to be told. Thus we find Aristeas, a Jew from Alexandria, who wrote his brother Philocrates an undated letter, approximately in 270 B.C., in which he told him how this translation was carried out. Everything indicates that there was no such thing as this letter, and it should be considered a legendary narration that cannot be taken literally. In short, it says the following:

Ptolemy King of Egypt had a fantastic library, but the Hebrew Scriptures were missing. In order to incorporate them, he summoned seventy-two scribes and sages of Israel—six for each tribe—to come to his kingdom and translate the scriptures into Greek. After an exchange of letters, Eleazar, the high priest of Jerusalem, selected the scribes and sent them to Alexandria to carry out the translation.

Once there, the king offered them a banquet lasting several days, asked each one a question, and was amazed by the answer given by each sage. Afterwards they were taken to the island of Pharos, facing Alexandria, where they carried out the work of translation. Every day they translated a portion and, when everyone agreed upon the text, the head of the group, called Demetrius, made a clean copy.

When the translation of the Pentateuch was finished, it was read before the people and then before the king. He was amazed by the depth of the wisdom of the Bible. Then he gave each translator fine clothes, two talents of gold and all kinds of presents to take to Israel upon their return. This is as far as the summary of the content of the letter goes.

Because there were seventy-two sages, it was called the Septuagint and is abbreviated as LXX. Over time, this version incorporated other books into the text that are known today as "apocryphal books" and are not part of our Old Testament, although some of them are accepted by the Catholic Church and are included in its Bible.

The Septuagint was the version used by Judaism outside of Israel for several centuries until the Apostle Paul and the Christian Gentiles read it as their first Bible, before the New Testament texts were compiled and added to the Old Testament.

Although Latin did not replace Greek as the language of Europe, this translation by the Jews in Egypt was the Scripture that the church used to spread the gospel.

(From the *Letter of Aristeas*, 47–50; 187–304)

Dinah, the Curious

WE WILL NOT OMIT this story from the Bible just because it is tragic. The worst part about it is that it involves good feelings, things that we would like to commend but that set off a spiral of violence and blood. It is chapter 34 of the Book of Genesis. The protagonist is called Dinah, the only daughter mentioned among the descendants of Jacob. We know very little about her, but we know something essential and marvelous: she was curious. And she wished to meet other women of her land. She left her village and went on the road in search of friends.

On the road, fate decreed that she cross paths with a pitiless man. Shechem raped her and then—to avoid punishment—said that he had fallen in love with her and asked her father for her hand in marriage. That is the beginning of the second tragedy. Dinah's brothers sought revenge and asked the men of Shechem to circumcise themselves as a condition for leaving Dinah with Shechem and, in addition, for the two peoples to live together and begin exchanging goods and women. They did so and, on the third day, when the wound from the circumcision had weakened them, two of Dinah's brothers, Simeon and Levi, attacked the town, killed all the men and took the women and children captive.

The Hebrew name Dinah is related to judgment and justice. The verb that means "to judge," the abstract noun "judgment" and the nouns *dan* and *dayyán*, both meaning "judge," derive from that name.

The proper name Dan ("judge") is the masculine form of Dinah. Perhaps we should not exaggerate these linguistic links, but it isn't a good idea to ignore them. This play on words is an invitation to delve into this tragic story in which a woman named Dinah is the victim of sexual violence and in which, in turn, this action unleashes a maelstrom of violence between two neighboring peoples that should have lived in harmony.

I know that these things are forbidden to us, but I would like to have a few minutes with Dinah to tell her the following: Don't stop being curious. Go out into the world to see what's behind the wall, how others live, what language they speak, what tastes are on their palate, what they long for. None of what was told here is your fault. Let us cry together for the women and children that your brothers took. And then get back to walking; there is a lot of land to be known.

(Genesis 34)

The First Passover

THE FIRST PASSOVER WAS that of the Israelite slaves in Egypt summoned to freedom by God. They were real slaves, subjected to forced labor, to exhausting work days, condemned not to be near their wives and children, the ones they most loved. God wished to deliver them from that slavery.

It is difficult to imagine the loneliness of a slave, of an enslaved community. For them there are no laws, no lawyers, and no reason to live. Their hearts beat, their intestines process what reaches them, but a slave's life is worth no more than the wealth he can produce for his master. The life of a slave is measured by his muscles and age. The older he is, the less he is worth.

Does he whose own body does not belong to him have the right to demand justice? Justice for whom? For this heart or this hand that belongs to another?

That is why it was not a complaint but a cry that burst from the enslaved people in Egypt. A complaint is directed at someone but a cry is what comes from the entrails of a person who suffers. It has no destination because it is not directed at anyone; it does not believe that there is anyone out there who will have pity for the pain and it does not believe that help is possible. It is the most tragic sound, without hope, without the belief that anyone will hear. A cry expresses senseless pain because there is nothing to justify that wound, yet it festers continuously like an endless caravan.

But God who never sleeps heard the cry of the slaves and began the task of transforming their reality. The text says that the cry rose up to God. And there were many things: there was a reunion between Aaron and his brother Moses who had fled long ago; there was dialogue with the pharaoh and there were plagues that hurt the earth. The next-to-last one sowed darkness over the country and took it back to the time before light had been created, the time of chaos and solitude. But the hardness of the pharaoh had no limits. The last plague decimated the population when the firstborn of the Egyptians died. The pharaoh's son, the heir to the throne, succumbed before the eyes of his father, who was powerless to stop the tragedy that extended throughout the people whom he claimed to protect.

Then came the hurried escape, the unleavened bread, the sea that opened to make way for the slaves who were seeking freedom.

The first Passover celebrated these acts of God.

(Exodus 2:23–25)

The First Coin

AT SOME POINT SOMEONE felt that it was inconvenient to cart sheep and grain in exchange for lumber and wine. Not only was it inconvenient, but they were perishable objects that, soon after delivery or reception, suffered the deterioration that comes with the passage of time. There was also another problem: at times it was very difficult to establish equivalency between cedar boards and flasks of oil, or between woven goods and clay vessels.

An anonymous genius—like the one who invented the zero—thought that the exchange of same-weight pieces of an incorruptible metal would allow a value to be established that would be a reference point for any items exchanged: that day was the day in which the coin was created.

This happened somewhere in the Near East, approximately in the 7th century B.C., some argue about whether it was in the city of Lydia, in present-day Turkey, or in the Greek island of Aegina. It was made of electrum, a natural alloy of gold and silver, and it began to circulate first around the island, then along the coast and finally throughout the entire known world.

The most ancient coins that we know of are engraved with a turtle, or a dolphin or a lion. Only later was the figure of the king engraved. It was thus that soon other kingdoms and cities began to mint their own coins, because each king wanted to see his own figure engraved on those small metal circles that everyone wanted to own and accumulate.

The daric was not the first coin but it might as well have been because it was the first to have international influence by being distributed throughout the entire Persian Empire. It was created by King Darius around 500 B.C. and was used until Alexander the Great conquered the empire, melted the darics and minted more drachmas—the Greek coin, which he needed for his campaigns. The daric weighed 8.4 grams of pure gold. It bore the image of a Persian King holding a bow and arrow, but has no inscription so it is not known which king it represents. For a long time it was thought that the name "daric" came from the Emperor Darius, but now we know that it comes from the Persian word *zarig*, which means "gold" or "shine."

In Israel, which was under the Persian Empire for two hundred years, the daric had widespread circulation, although it is only mentioned twice: when Ezra counted the gifts of King Cyrus for the reconstruction of the temple (Ezra 8:27) and when David collected funds to build the temple (1 Chronicles 29:7). But this last mention is an anachronism, since David lived 400 years before the coin was invented. No doubt in his time the donors gave spices and the author of Chronicles converted the value to darics so his contemporaries could understand the magnitude of the offering.

(From Roland de Vaux,
Old Testament Institutions, II, 13, 5)

Mary David Allen, the Birth

THE STRANGE NAME (MARY David, used and pronounced together) hides a story. There were two moments on two separate days that marked the lives of those who experienced them. The memory of those lightning bolts in time—and their mystery, which only God knows—persists in the name. We met her in Dallas, Texas. She tells us the story, and it is the story of her birth in 1930.

> "Two years before I was born, my parents and my siblings returned from China, where my father had been a Methodist missionary for several years. They settled in South Carolina, where he remained throughout the rest of his ministry. It was Christmas of 1929 and my mother, already nearing forty years of age, was four months pregnant. That day they decided to take the entire family on a ride and on the road a wheel came off of the automobile, the vehicle turned over and Mother fell out, hitting the ground. She was the most injured and as a result of the impact her body was paralyzed from the neck down. Her muscles did not respond; she could only speak and move her eyes. Days and months went by, and Mary—that was her name—did not recover from the accident and her physical condition began to deteriorate. In mid-April the doctors decided to perform an emergency cesarean, perhaps because they felt that her condition was deteriorating at an increasing rate and that her life would not last through all nine months of the pregnancy. They scheduled the intervention for the next day."

That is when the unexpected occurred, what marked her for life. Mary David continued with her story.

> "On the next day, a few hours before going to the operating room, my mother went into labor, with her entire body still paralyzed and her muscles inert. The baby pushed and the muscles responded. The doctors could not understand how, but they allowed her body to work. After a few moments a girl was born by natural childbirth. At delivery, due to excessive blood loss, a transfusion was required and her nephew, named David, contributed his blood."

> "The baby was called Mary David, after my mother and my cousin. I have used both names together all my life. Mother died less than one month after I was born."

Martin Luther King, Your Dream, Our Dream

For Aldo Etchegoyen

DARK SKIN WAS DIRTY; white skin was clean. Dark skin meant ignorance; white skin meant knowledge and the right to power. Black skin had to reverence light skin, give up the seat on the bus, not use its bathrooms, not attend the same school nor sing together in the same church. Black children were not allowed to play with white kids. Dark skin was the mark of sin.

Martin Luther King dreamed that someday that would end in his country and in the world.

He was a Baptist pastor in the Deep South of the United States. He preached the gospel of the love of God every time he was given a pulpit. And in his sermons, the love of God was an invitation for each believer to love his neighbor in a real and effective manner the way he was, and with the skin color that God had given him. The love of God for his creatures meant that we should celebrate as a gift from God—not lament—that there should be white and black persons. He preached that we not only have to favor and do good, but that we have the obligation to oppose evil with all our might. He said with the strength of a prophet that it is not enough to be fair and honest in our personal relationships; we had the duty to fight against injustice and work for the end of discrimination and racial hatred in our society.

He was a disciple of Henry Thoreau and Gandhi. Like them, he proclaimed that civil disobedience was a powerful tool for opposing abuse and humiliation. He did not doubt that law had to be respected; but if unfair, there is no obligation to obey it. The fact that in his marches he demanded things as elementary as the right to vote, the abolition of segregation laws and the right to a salary similar to that of whites, reveal the extent of the racist disease of the society of his day.

In order to prevent such basic rights, Black community churches were burned, their leaders' houses were destroyed, children were murdered, crowds were machine-gunned and thousands of persons were imprisoned. Terrorist madness was unleashed to prevent a Black woman from traveling on the same train as her White brethren, a Black child from learning the alphabet next to his White friend, Black men and White women or White men and Black women from falling in love and dancing to the same rhythm. Martin Luther King responded to that violence with nonviolence.

Pastor King was assassinated in the city of Memphis, Tennessee on April 4, 1968. He was there to support the strike by local Black garbage collectors who were demanding salaries equal to those of their White coworkers. What he called the second stage of the struggle for civil rights and dubbed the "Poor People's Campaign," had begun. This campaign was to include all the poor. In his words: "It should not just be Black people, but all poor people. We must include Indians, Puerto Ricans, Mexicans, even poor Whites." He demanded justice, education and decent work for his country's poor.

Some of his dreams have now come true; others are still waiting. His life is an invitation to dream with him, that reality can be changed by our actions, and that the violence of the powerful can be defeated.

The Ten Commandments

THE TEN COMMANDMENTS (OR "ten words" according to the Hebrew text) are found in two places of the Old Testament. We read them in Exodus 20:1–17 and we find them once again in Deuteronomy 5:5–21. The two versions are almost identical, but we would like to mention two aspects that usually go unnoticed by readers.

The first is that we speak of "ten" commandments, although there are actually fourteen. If we count the imperative negative words ("you shall not. . .") in the list of commandments, we find twelve; to these we must add two commandments in positive form (referring to resting on the Sabbath and proper respect for parents), which gives us a total fourteen times on which God indicates a given conduct. This is the list:

1. You shall not have any other gods.
2. You shall not make idols or images.
3. You shall not bow down to them.
4. You shall not honor them.
5. You shall not take the name of the Lord your God in vain.
6. Remember the Sabbath to keep it holy.
7. You shall not do any work on it [the Sabbath].
8. Honor your father and your mother.
9. You shall not kill.

10. You shall not commit adultery.

11. You shall not steal.

12. You shall not bear false witness against your neighbor.

13. You shall not covet your neighbor's house.

14. You shall not covet your neighbor's wife.

It is probable that originally, there were ten negative commandments—hence the name—to which two more were added to reach the symbolic number twelve and, finally, the two "positive" commandments were incorporated. Actually, it does not matter how many there are, but that they were given as superior laws to organize the life of the people.

The second is that there is only one difference between the two versions, and it concerns the commandment about keeping the Sabbath. This is one of the commandments that include their foundation, and that is where we find the difference. While Exodus 20:11 is based on imitating the day on which the Lord rested after finishing the Creation, Deuteronomy 5:15 indicates that the Sabbath rest evokes the liberation from slavery in Egypt. To what is this change due?

There are several possible answers, but the one that seems most fitting has to do with the public to which the two texts is directed. In chapter 26 of the Book of Numbers, a census of the Israelites takes place, at the end of which (vv. 63–64) it was said: "But among these there was not one man of those numbered by Moses and Aaron the priest, who had numbered the people of Israel in the wilderness of Sinai." Thus, those who went out of Egypt had already died and are distinguished from the new generation consisting of those who were born in the desert and had not known the time of slavery. As of Numbers 27, the text of the Pentateuch is directed to the "generation of the wilderness," men and women who looked toward the future with hope but had to be instructed in the teachings of the past.

The audience of Exodus was made up of freed slaves who did not need to be reminded of the meaning of slavery and freedom.

The Sabbath rest was a gift from God, for they knew the reality of forced labor and the cruelty of Pharaoh's chieftains. For the new generation—bred on manna from heaven and abundant quail—the risk of forgetting where they came from was great and dangerous. The second version of the Decalogue is meant for them; they are taught that the day of rest is an occasion to "remember that you were a slave in Egypt." It is said in the present for them to know that it is part of their own history.

Delilah, the Woman Samson Loved

EVERYTHING INDICATES THAT SHE was a Philistine. Samson the warrior, the strong, saw her in the Valley of Sorek and fell in love with her. Delilah must have been very beautiful, although the story says nothing about her beauty. What the story does reveal is her courage, her intelligence, and her ability to handle a complex and dangerous situation. Also, her knowledge of male psychology. We would have preferred for her to use that sum of abilities for another purpose; but our mission is not to judge the story but to tell it. The facts are narrated in the sixteenth chapter of the Book of Judges. We summarize it here in order to make our own conclusions. This is the story of Delilah and Sampson.

When the Philistines find out that Delilah is living with Sampson and that he is in love with her, they come up with a plan. The Philistines know that a man in love is capable of any nonsense for his woman, and that Sampson is no exception. They offer her eleven hundred pieces of silver, an immense amount of money, for her to use her wiles to discover the secret of his strength.

Delilah begins the task of piercing into her lover's conscience to retrieve the secret. Three times Delilah asks, and as many times Sampson answers without telling her the true cause of his strength. The third time, Delilah bursts into tears and uses the most subtle and powerful argument; sobbing to the point of dehydration, she gasps: "You say you love me, but your heart is not with me; you

Delilah, the Woman Samson Loved

have deceived me three times and you won't tell me the secret of your strength."

We can imagine the scene: Delilah shedding tears and demanding openness in line with the love that he professes for her and that she gives in return, and Sampson unable to make up his mind because he loves this woman but is afraid to reveal his secret. During the next few days, she insists and he gets distressed. He thinks that, if he loves her, why not tell her his secret; if they get along so well, why not share his most intimate thoughts with her. Sampson hesitates—perhaps remembering that she is a Philistine. But his mind gives in and darkens; and love in intimacy is stronger than the brain. Sampson opens his heart to Delilah and tells her that the secret of his strength is in his hair.

We know how the story ends. Delilah first gets her money and then has Sampson fall asleep on her knees. Unconscious, he allows his hair to be cut and when Sampson wakes up, he is weakened and easily taken captive. We know nothing more of Delilah, who disappears from the narration and is never mentioned again.

In Delilah we find cleverness and sagacity at the service of infidelity and deceit. Delilah is very human; she accepts the bribe, the same one we are offered every day and are called upon not to accept.

(Judges 16)

Another Love Story
Rebekah and Isaac

THINGS WERE DIFFERENT IN Abraham's time. The father was concerned about finding a wife for his son Isaac but he had his conditions. She couldn't come from Canaan, but from his own land, the region of Nahor; yet Isaac could not go to Nahor; he had to stay in Canaan. It was a complicated matter, so he called a servant and commissioned him to go to those lands in search of a wife for his son Isaac.

The servant took ten camels, a group of companions and gifts of the highest quality, and set out in a caravan to find the young woman. The servant also had his own methods for identifying her. He thought: "If I ask her for water and she gives it to me, and then she says that she will also water my camels, then that's her! If not, she is not the woman I'm seeking." That would be the sign. When he reached the doors of Nahor, he saw a young virgin come out with a jar on her shoulder. It was Rebekah, and Rebekah was beautiful. The servant approached and asked for water... She gave him a drink and said, "I will also draw water for your camels."

The servant was bursting with joy. The girl must not have understood what was happening, especially not when the stranger put a ring in her nose and two bracelets of pure gold on her arms.

Then the servant explained his mission to the young woman's family and how he had arrived there looking for Abraham's relatives. Her father Bethuel, her brother Laban and everyone else were very happy, particularly to find out that they had a rich relative and that the daughter would be marrying his only heir.

But feelings are not that simple: her mother and Laban—who realized they would not see Rebekah again, asked for her to stay with them ten more years. Since the servant insisted on not delaying, they decided to consult Rebekah. Anxious to marry, to discover a new world and to expand in another land, she did not hesitate to ask to leave that same day, for she understood that there was no conflict between her love of her family and the attraction of the unknown.

The rest of the story can be summed up as follows: when they were nearing Abraham's house, Rebekah saw a young man from afar. Almost at the same time, Isaac lifted his eyes and crossed glances with Rebekah. She, still from afar, asked: "Who is that?" and the servant answered, "It is he who awaits you." Chaste and delicate, she covered her face with her veil. Then Isaac received her and they went to his tent. Rebekah and Isaac loved each other from that day on, for the rest of their lives.

(Genesis 24)

Huldah, the Prophetess

THE MASONS AND CRAFTSMEN who repaired the temple of Jerusalem found the scroll of the Law among the rubble. They quickly took it to Hilkiah, the High Priest, who took it to Shaphan, the King's secretary. He read it and took it to King Josiah. When the King heard the words written on the scroll, he ripped his clothes, begged for mercy and asked his secretaries to consult God about the truth of what it contained. The distance between the Word of God and the behavior of the people was so great that if everything it said was true, Israel's days were counted. Consulting God meant consulting the prophets.

Every patriarchal society reserves its best positions, those that come with prestige and power, for men. Ancient Israel was no exception, but on this occasion they consulted the prophetess Huldah. We do not know what her husband Shallum, who was a palace employee, thought, but he might have thought that his job depended on what his wife said. We cannot speculate about that, but nothing held Huldah back, and she confirmed the King's worst fears concerning the future of Israel and also added that the King would die young.

Three things stand out in this story. First, is the high esteem in which the King held this prophetess. His secretaries and the High Priest did not hesitate to consult her to authenticate the scroll they had just found and, when they heard her words, no one questioned her condition as a prophetess of the Lord.

Huldah, the Prophetess

Second, is that unlike other prophets and prophetesses, Huldah had the courage to announce a message that might irritate the King and the authorities, and even pit her against high government officials and military chiefs. Some had lost their lives for prophesying as she did.

Third, is the essential concern that the account gives no indication that a woman prophet was out of the ordinary in those days. Nothing leads us to believe the contrary. The fact is not emphasized, but rather is presented naturally without anyone being surprised by it. A unique case, a woman that bent men to her will by her sagacity, would have deserved praise whose effect would have been to diminish the worth of women: only her brilliance would justify a woman exercising that office. But Huldah does not appear to be any more apt than her male coworkers; she was simply called to be God's spokesperson, although being a woman.

What we regret is that we have only this brief episode of her prophecy; we would have liked a whole book on Huldah testifying of her wisdom and message.

(2 Kings 22:11–20 and 2 Chronicles 23:22–28)

The Days from October 5 to 14, 1582 Do Not Exist

THAT IS CORRECT. Up to then the Julian calendar had been used, the one that Emperor Julius Caesar had commissioned in the year 45 B.C. That emperor asked the sage Sosigenes to organize the calendar because, with the one they used, over time the dates shifted in relation to the yearly seasons.

Sosigenes made his calculations and it turned out that the solar year lasted 365 days and six hours. So it was established that one day (the sum of six hours per year) would be added every four years so that there would be no discrepancy between the calendar and the arrival of the seasons. That is how leap year was born, the one that falls every four years and has one day added to the month of February.

But time passes, the Earth spins and things did not go as planned. As it happens, the calculation was not so accurate, since the Earth circles the sun in 365 days, five hours, 48 minutes and 45 seconds. Those twelve minutes and 45 seconds might not seem like much, but the difference added up year after year and, in the 14th century, the discrepancy between the calendar and the seasons was very obvious: there was a ten-day difference. By then there was no longer an emperor who governed the entire world, but there were Popes and they were concerned about the liturgical calendar and setting the date for the Christian Easter. As a result, Pope Gregory XIII had the calendar adjusted to the Earth's actual path in its

The Days from October 5 to 14, 1582 Do Not Exist

pilgrimage around the Sun in order to set the dates of the religious calendar correctly.

Following arduous consultations with astronomers and by indication of the wise man Lilius, he decided to remove ten days from the almanac and established that Friday, October 5, 1582 should be called Friday, October 15, continuing the dates from there as if nothing had happened. The almanac was thus corrected. And to avoid future discrepancies, it was also established that one leap year should be skipped every four hundred years. In conclusion, those ten days never existed.

However, not everyone agreed that the Church of Rome had the authority to decide which day we live in and when national holidays and birthdays should be celebrated. It took some time before it was applied in many countries, which meant that two calendars were in use simultaneously in Europe and its colonies. For example, in Germany and the Netherlands, it was not used until the year 1700. England and its colonies adopted it in 1752, Alaska in 1867, Russia in 1918 and Greece in 1923.

At that time Phillip II ruled Spain and, due to the difficulties in communicating the new date to places as remote as Cartagena de Indias or Lima, or the end of the Earth where there was a little village they called Buenos Aires, he decided to postpone the change for a year, so in the American viceroyalties the almanac was changed on October 5, 1583. As a result, in this part of the world October 5–15 existed in 1582 but not in 1583.

It is said that Miguel de Cervantes and William Shakespeare died on the same day, April 23, 1616. To be exact, we would have to say that Cervantes died a few hours earlier, on the 22nd. But actually, Shakespeare died ten days later, although their almanacs and death certificates bear the same date: Spain was using the Gregorian calendar and England the Julian one.

The Year in Which We Live

This year is the year 1620 of the Byzantine Era.

The year 2061 of the Julian Calendar.

The year 5775 of the Jewish Calendar.

The year 2790 of the Greek Olympic Era.

The year 2768 *Ab urbe condita*, which means "since the foundation of the city," that is, since the foundation of Rome. It is the Roman Calendar.

The year 2641 of the era of Nabopolassar, founder of the Neobabilonian Empire.

The year 2675 according to the Imperial Calendar of the Japanese Era, still in use.

The year 2015 of the Soviet Revolutionary Calendar, with six weeks of five days each for every month, established in 1929 and abandoned in 1940.

The year 2052 of the Hispanic Era, imposed by Octavian Augustus after conquering Hispania, used in Portugal until the fifteenth century.

The year 2327 of the Greek or Seleucid Era, preserved in Syria.

The year 223 of the French Republic Calendar, abolished by Napoleon I in 1805.

The year 1731 of the Diocletian Era, used by the Ethiopians and Egyptian Copts.

The Year in Which We Live

The year 1393 of the Hijrah, the Islamic Calendar.

The year 4713 of the Chinese Calendar.

The year 2015 of the Christian Era.

The Origin of Writing

THE PLACE IS LOWER Mesopotamia, between the Euphrates and Tigris rivers, where their waters converge and form the delta that pours into the Persian Gulf. The people are called Sumerians by their enemies the Acadians, but they call themselves *sag-giga*, which means "people of black heads." The time is that of the hot sun and fertile rivers during the years around 3500 B.C. Geography did not give these people solid stones with which to build their cities or metals for their instruments. It gave them abundant clay and with it they invented bricks which, baked or unbaked, allowed them to build everything they needed to become a powerful and cultured nation. It also gave them wood for their farming and musical instruments.

It is always exciting to imagine the first gesture, the first line. Someone took a splinter and drew a hand, a sun, an eye or a mountain on a brick that was still damp. Maybe he or she then saw that a bit of clay could be given to someone else and transmit something through those drawings. An experience ("it is hot"), a feeling ("I like your eyes"), an intention ("I give you my hand"), a proposal ("let's go to the mountain"). On that day, that man or woman invented writing. With time, the splinter became a length of cane with a wedge-shaped point and the brick became a clay tablet made to be written on. When they wished to preserve the writing, they baked it and placed it in the library. This writing is called "cuneiform" or "wedge-shaped" because it is written with a wedge.

The Origin of Writing

At first they were ideograms. They represented what was drawn: serpent, tree, grains. But it was soon understood that as many drawings as there are things would be needed, and that was impractical and perhaps impossible. Then, in order to simplify, they began to give sounds to the signs: at first each sign was a syllable. One sign for "ca," another for "ra" and another for "van." The word "caravan" could be written with these three signs or letters. More words could be formed with other signs (ta, mi, co, su, la, etc.), and they were interchanged and combined to expand writing. Approximately seventy or eighty syllable signs were enough to write almost any word.

When they invented writing, the Sumerians inaugurated the recording of facts, that is, history. Ancient religious narrations, legends and myths began to be preserved with this system. Recipes for cooking and recipes for making medicines were recorded. Palaces, streets and cities were described. Marriage, rental and property contracts came into being. Kings published their laws and decrees; generals reported on their battles.

All of this went to the library and slept under the ground for over 4000 years. It was not until the late 19th century that the existence of this culture was discovered, and even more time was needed to decipher the writings and to read the thousands of tablets of baked clay of its libraries. Since then, we have come to know that it was the Sumerians who invented reading and writing. They also created the first school. A Sumerian story relates this dialogue between teacher and student:

"What have you done at school?" asks the teacher.

"I have read my tablet; I have worked on my new tablet and I have covered it with writing," replies the child.

The Hebrew Letters and Their Predecessors

CHANGING THE LETTERS WITH which their sacred writings are produced would appear to be an unthinkable cultural change for a people to whom they are an agglutinating and devotional element. However, when the Israelites returned from the Babylonian captivity in the year 539 B.C. they brought with them a new alphabet to replace the writing used for centuries by their ancestors.

The alphabet we know today as Hebrew, the so-called *square* writing that we see in the synagogues, religious texts and the Hebrew Bible, and which is used to write today in Israel, is not the original Hebrew writing, but is of Aramaic origin. The more ancient one from Israel itself is called Paleo-Hebrew (that is, Old Hebrew), a writing related to the Phoenician alphabet. Due to its antiquity, only Paleo-Hebrew texts written in hard materials like ceramic or stone have survived. The most ancient inscriptions we have in Paleo-Hebrew are the alphabet (*alephat*) of Tel Zait and the calendar of Gezer, both engraved on stone and dating from the 10th century B.C. The Mesha Stele is an extensive text on basaltic stone from the 8th century B.C. Another one is the inscription of Siloam which narrates the construction in Jerusalem of the water canal that bears its name and was built during the reign of King Hezekiah (716–687; 2 Kings 20:20), a stone that is now on exhibition in the Archeological Museum of Istanbul.

So, for some unknown reason, they abandoned a prestigious ancient writing of their own and adopted another one, of foreign origin. But the adoption of the new writing was not an act without its mark on the politics and religion of Israel. The name Judah was engraved with Paleo-Hebrew letters on the coins minted during the time of the Maccabees (first and second centuries B. C.) and the Judaic wars, and many of the Qumran manuscripts, which date from the same time, have the name Yahve (in many Bibles written *Jehovah*) engraved in the ancient Hebrew letters.

The most extensive document that has survived in Paleo-Hebrew is the Pentateuch that is preserved to this day by the Samaritan community. It is the only sacred text of this community, and its mere existence suggests that the change in writing was understood as a cultural concession to the Persian government and a subjugation of their own tradition.

Therefore ancient Hebrew writing was not forgotten and certain Jewish groups used it to indicate political or theological differences with the official leadership. Could this indicate that the change of writing was imposed by the Persian imperial authority? Or that the leadership of Israel did it and then imposed it on its people as a gesture of friendship toward the empire, to ingratiate themselves with the new masters of the world?

We do not know, but the fact that it persisted as an act of resistance in the Maccabean coins, in the letters with which the name of God was written in Qumran or among the Samaritans, leads us to believe that the new writing was not easily assimilated and that for some it was viewed as foreign and linked to imperial power. It also reveals that the letters we use say more than the sounds they represent.

Our Alphabet

From the Phoenicians to Our Times

THE LONG ROAD TO our current twenty-seven letter of the Spanish alphabet (but twenty –six in the English alphabet), is a sign of its complexity. We have already mentioned that it all began in Sumer, where writing was invented in the middle of the fourth millennium before Christ.

The original symbols gave way to syllabic writing and, toward the 14th century, we find in Ugarit, on the coast of what is now Lebanon, the first alphabetic writing in which each sign represents a single sound. It took 2000 years to perfect a system that is able to write any word with just a handful of symbols. The Semitic alphabet (Hebrew, Canaanite, etc.) has 22 letters and all words can be written with them.

The people who spread this alphabet throughout the Mediterranean world were the Phoenicians. Together with their trade and sea culture, their letters reached everywhere. And in what interests us, it reached Greece, where the Greeks adopted it to write their own language. It should be noted that a Semitic alphabet was used to write a language that was not Semitic but Indo-European. And this required certain adjustments. The most striking one is that while the Phoenician alphabet had no symbols for vowels, the Greeks needed them. So they used the Semitic letters for sounds that they did not use for the vowels. For example, the guttural letter *aleph* was used for the *a* (alpha); the Phoenician letter *he* was used for the *e* (epsilon); another guttural, *ayin* indicated the

Our Alphabet

o (omicron). The Greeks copied the Phoenician letters, made the Greek alphabet, and during their expansion took it to the coasts of what is now Italy. The Etruscans lived there; they adopted it and spread it throughout the peninsula. Over time it evolved into what we now call the "Latin alphabet," that is, our own.

All languages derived from Latin were written with the letters used to write this page. As European culture spread, these letters were incorporated into the writings of other peoples, who used them because of their simplicity and versatility for adapting to the sounds of almost any language. Christianity is not innocent of this process. Wherever the Roman Church prevailed, the Latin alphabet reigned (Slavic languages like Croatian, Polish, Czech and others adopted it); where the Orthodox Church prevailed, the Cyrillic alphabet reigned (Russian, Ukrainian, Belarusian, Bosnian). The Cyrillic alphabet is a writing created by Saint Cyril in the 9th century, also based on the Greek letters.

In any event, each Romance language indicated its particularities with accents and some letters of their own. Portuguese included the ç; French its three accents and the ligatures æ and œ; Rumanian the ș and the ț. The emerging Spanish of the Lower Middle Ages added the ñ, a letter that is now threatened by computer globalization. It must be defended, because while it would not be a bad idea to do without *cañones* (cannons), *engaños* (deceits) and *riñas* (fighting), it would be sad if we stopped warming ourselves in winter with *leña* (wood), no longer enjoyed *castañas* (chestnuts) or, what would be more serious and deadly, if we abandoned *sueños* (dreams) and *soñar* (dreaming).

Luke, the Writer

LUKE IS MENTIONED THREE times in the New Testament in Paul's epistles, and that is why he is considered to be his friend and collaborator. In the 2nd century, it was Irenaeus who attributed the second Gospel and the book of Acts to Luke, although his name is not mentioned in either of these works. We do not know if it was Paul's friend Luke—or someone else—who wrote these two books, but at any rate, we do know that their author was a Gentile, did not know Jesus in person, and wrote the Gospel and the book of Acts as a witness of what he received from others and of what he had in part experienced with Paul. Perhaps he wrote other things, but only these books remain of his works.

Both narrations are addressed to his friend Theophilus, as stated at the beginning of each one, a person we know nothing about, and who might be a literary fiction, since his name means "friend of God." It says there that others had already written about "this story" and that he is writing "an orderly account" of the things that happened in Jesus' life and afterwards in the early Christian communities. He was probably referring to the fact that there were loose fragments about the acts and words of Jesus, which he was now seeking to organize in a linear and coherent manner. He was an eminent writer and his narrations carry the mark of good prose that lingers on details but also knows how to get to the heart of things.

Lucas was a Gentile and a physician. Our present-day knowledge was not available to the physicians of that day, but they made

Luke, the Writer

do with the medicines of the time: sometimes they recommended wine as a cure (1 Timothy 5:23). For many, medicine was a divine gift and those who exercised it did not charge for their services. We do not know if Luke earned his living as a physician, but the fact that he traveled with Paul—at least he was with him as of the second journey—is an indication that he did not devote himself exclusively to healing the sick.

Luke's thinking and that of the Apostle Paul are very close on some subjects. Both liked to call Jesus "Lord" and both offer a very similar account of the institution of the Last Supper. Both—and this is important because Luke was a Gentile—emphasized the equality of Jews and Gentiles in the new community of the Church. However, there are those who think that the writer and Paul's friend were not the same person and that the connection was only established later. In truth, given the information we have, we cannot affirm one or the other.

We know nothing of his last days. Christian tradition has established that he died a martyr in the Greek city of Patras or in Rome.

Jewish Wisdom I

Body, Soul and Judgment

EMPEROR ANTONIUS SAID TO Rabbi Yehudah HaNasi: Body and soul can escape judgment. How? The body can say: "It is the soul that sinned, since from the day it left I have been lying in the tomb, as unmoving as a stone. And the soul can say: It is the body that has sinned, since from the day I separated from it, I have been soaring in the sky, free as a bird."

Rabbi Yehudah HaNasi replied: This can be compared to the following story: A king of flesh and blood had a garden and in it grew very appetizing figs. He set two guardians to care for them: one was crippled and the other was blind. Then the cripple said to the blind man: I see some very appetizing figs in the garden. Go and put me on your shoulders; then I will cut them and we will eat them.

A few days later, the owner of the garden arrived and said, "Where are my figs?"

The cripple said, "Do I have legs to get to them?"

The blind man said, "Do I have eyes to see them?"

What did the king do? He put the cripple on top of the blind man and judged them as one. So He, blessed be His name, takes the soul and pours it over the body, and judges them as one.

(From *Talmud Bavli, Sanhedrin,* 91a)

Jewish Wisdom II

What Good is Bread?

Rabbi Elazar ben Azariah says:
What good is respect if there is no Torah? But if we lack respect, our Torah is no longer important.

If there is no wisdom, there can be no fear of God; but if there is no fear of God, what good is our wisdom?

If there is no science, there is no intelligence; but if there is no intelligence, what good is science?

If there is no bread, there is no study; but if there is no study, what good is bread?

(From *Talmud Bavli, Pirkei Avot*, 3, 1)

Jewish Wisdom III

The Emperor and the Rabbi

HADRIAN, EMPEROR OF ROME, told Rabbi Joshua ben Hananiah: "I am worth more than your Master Moshe, because a live dog is worth more than a dead lion."

The rabbi replied: "Moshe is an exception to that rule, as I will prove to you. Proclaim a decree requiring that no fire be lit in Rome tomorrow."

The Emperor so decreed. On the next day, he went to the palace terrace with the rabbi to see if there was any smoke in the city. After a while they saw smoke coming out of a chimney. An investigation was ordered and the Emperor was informed that a citizen was ill and his physician had ordered him to drink hot water.

"You see," said the rabbi. "You forbid lighting fire for a single day and your order was disobeyed for a banal reason. Moshe forbid lighting fire fifty two days a year (every *Shabbat*) and he has been scrupulously obeyed for centuries, unless a life is in danger."

(From *Kohelet Raba*, 9, 4)

Jewish Wisdom IV

A Man Travels Through the Desert

A MAN WAS TRAVELING through the desert. He was hungry, thirsty and tired when he found a tree that provided abundant shade, delicious fruit, and a spring ran under it.

The man ate the fruit, drank the water and rested in the shade.

When he was ready to resume his journey he turned toward the tree and said:

"Tree, how shall I bless you? Shall I bless you with sweet fruit? Your fruit is already sweet. Shall I bless you with abundant shade? Your shade is already abundant. Shall I ask for a spring to run under you? A spring is already running under you. There is only one thing with which I can bless you: may it be God's will for all the trees that come from your seed to be like you."

(From *Talmud Bavli, Taanit*, 5b)

Sex and the Bible I

OF THE TWO BIBLE stories about the creation of human beings, the first one says that God created them "male and female" and told them to join together sexually in order to multiply. He created them on the sixth day, together with the greater animals, establishing a fellowship that it took humanity centuries to discover, until the works of Charles Darwin made them evident. It also says that he created them "in His image," an expression that differentiates them from seals and lizards by giving them a gift that was denied to these: to be the creators of culture. Languages, cities, music, philosophies and roads would arise from their hands and thought. They would sculpt stone and wood; they would work the earth; they would design jewels to adorn themselves; they would cook their food; they would reproduce on walls the bulls they saw running through the prairie.

In the second account, we are told that He created an "earthly" being (that is what *adam* means), from the dust of the earth, who was not sexed, and we are confused if we think it was male. But it is not possible that God created a being with useless genitals. Let us imagine Adam asking himself when he found no use for his virile member: what is *this* for?

After a time, God decided to create Eve, and from then on we have a sexed couple that we can call male and female. "Bone of my bones, and flesh of my flesh," exclaimed the new male and felt for her something he had not experienced until then. She was a lot like him but different, and what he liked was the difference. She also, perhaps with wonder, perceived that what she most liked about him, was their difference.

The process of humanization was slow. Modesty was born after the limits imposed during Creation were transgressed: they did not feel comfortable displaying their bodies and they looked for leaves and covered themselves. Intimacy appeared and, with it, the game of showing and hiding to court the other. With this act, it became established that the exercise of sexuality would be a private act that likes closed spaces and flees from curious looks.

Because of that feeling that dwells deep inside, biblical narrations are little given to being explicit on the subject of sexuality. With the exception of the Song of Solomon, almost everything related to sexual relations is assumed. Of course modesty does not mean abstinence, and the stories themselves give proof that in a few generations and with great enthusiasm our ancestors populated the Earth with sons and daughters.

(Genesis 1—2)

Sex and the Bible II

IT IS A MIRACLE that the Song of Solomon is in the Bible. There was an attempt to remove it because it does not mention God and because there were those that thought that eroticism had no place in a book born of faith that proclaims the belief that good will triumph in the end. For them, sex and good were not friends. But there were those who defended it because they thought that love and sexuality deserved a place in the Bible.

The images are conclusive: The young man says "the mountain of myrrh" and the "hill of frankincense," both in the singular, which are images of exotic and aromatic places that resemble her sexual organs. What complicates the interpretation is that in other poems the plural "hills" is used so that it seems to allude to places in which pleasure between two can be freely experienced. We should not forget that "hills" may also be images of the breasts or repeated curves of the female body.

When reading love poems it is not necessary for every word to make a clear reference; the important thing is the mood created and the recurrence of images. To say that a gazelle roams over the hill easily, evokes the image of the man's hand running over her body and caressing it.

The young woman doesn´t stay behind, and speaks of how sweet he is, how he caresses her, his palate. She asks him to kiss her and says that, at times, she swoons with ecstasy.

For many readers a problem is that the Song does not talk about sex; neither is it a reflection; it does not give advice, nor says what is right or wrong, nor what can be done and what cannot. It is not a manual on sexuality nor a collection of laws that regulate it. The Song limits itself to telling the experience of two young people who love each other and therefore join sexually. They enjoy their bodies and hide in order not to be discovered, and to avoid being seen by others. As a literary work, it follows the line of saying without saying, of presenting an idea from a description of the facts. They lead the reader to a place where he or she is told what is happening and is left to draw his own conclusions.

The Song is like an extension of the Creation story in Genesis. There we are told how the first couple was created male and female. Here we see the consequences.

The Apostle Paul

OF ALL THE WRITERS of the New Testament, Paul is the most prolific, comparable only to Luke. Thirteen epistles are attributed to him and, although several of them might not have been written personally by Paul, his thinking and his particular perspective of the Gospel and of the person of Jesus are present with more or less force, even in the latter.

He was born in Tarsus, in the province of Cilicia, present-day Turkey. His family named him Saul, after the first king of Israel. The family was well-off and gave him a first-class Jewish education. As a family of Pharisees, they taught their son to read the Sacred Scriptures in Hebrew and to observe the religious rites and customs of their tradition. Later, in Jerusalem, he was a disciple of Gamaliel, a prestigious Pharisee doctor of the Law and grandson of Hillel the Elder, the great rabbi who renewed the Jewish thought of his day. With him, Paul delved deep into the Jewish traditions and grew in appreciation of the Greek culture.

As an adult, at the time of Stephen's martyrdom, Paul watched the events developing from afar and was honored by those who testified against this Christian martyr. This indicates that by then he was known for his zeal in persecuting Jews who accepted that Jesus of Nazareth was the expected Messiah. For even though they understood that being a good Jew meant accepting Jesus, Paul considered that, by accepting him, they perverted the faith of Israel. A crucified messiah was blasphemy, because a crucified person was considered cursed by God and abandoned to fate. For Paul, if

Jesus had been the Messiah, he would have been protected by God, not abandoned, as he himself stated on the cross. His humiliating death, was proof enough that he was an impostor.

However, the paths of men are not those of God. On his way to the city of Damascus, he was blinded by a powerful light while a voice called his name. That was the day he converted to the faith of the Messiah who had died and resurrected. From that moment onwards, he went from persecuting the believers to promoting faith in Jesus Christ, the Son of God.

Of Paul we must say that he put all his intellectual resources at the service of the Word. He knew like few others the Jewish culture that he inherited from his parents, and the Greek culture in which he was educated and dominated the world of his time. He had the ability to communicate with simple folk, to whom he preached in the synagogues of every town in which he arrived. And he was able to discuss with philosophers and scientists at the Aeropagus in Athens and in the circles of Roman thinkers.

It happened with him as with so many others. He met Jesus and his life changed forever.

The Mishnah and the Talmud

THE TALMUD IS THE compilation of several centuries of Jewish thinking, grouped by subject. The first thing written was the Mishnah, a work in which Rabbi Yehuda HaNasi organized hundreds of legal statements and decisions issued from the "oral Torah," thus called to distinguish it from the "written Torah" given to Moses on Mount Sinai (the Pentateuch). He organized it into six general treatises (on agriculture, feasts, women, crime, worship and ritual purity), which in turn were divided into chapters that treated the issues in greater detail. The Mishnah was completed around the year 200 of our era.

In the following years, the Mishnah was studied at the rabbinical schools. The system consisted in reading and discussing several paragraphs with the disciples, thus accumulating dialogues, discussions and conclusions on the subjects treated in its pages. Some rabbis became very famous and their opinions transcended the borders of their own schools. Thus the time arrived to record all that wealth of reflection and wisdom. As a result of all that, the Talmud was born.

The Talmud Bavli (the most consulted) was written in Babylon between the years 200 and 500. It follows the six-treatise structure of the Mishnah and adds to it the discussions and opinions that took place in the schools. The layout of its pages hold a particular characteristic that causes amazement to this day. The paragraph from the Mishnah is placed in the center in large letters, with the opinions of two of the greatest Jewish thinkers—Rashi to the right and Maimonides to the left—and those of other thinkers of the time, below.

A chain process can be seen in this work: the Talmud is based on the Mishnah, which in turn is based on the Torah. The most important work of Judaism after the Bible came from this way of thinking. Although the Talmud is a finished work, it continues to generate new reflections and thoughts. In fact, there is a great deal of literature after the Talmud that comments and completes it. But just as new works arise, others are also forgotten, although the Talmud remains as the central document of the Jewish tradition.

The Talmud has the nebulous prestige of having been defamed, consigned to fire and humiliated. Those who created it knew what they were doing. A Jewish community that stops studying the Talmud loses one of the columns of its existence.

Psalms, the Bible Hymnbook

CHURCHES GROUP SONGS INTO volumes that we call hymn books. They hold the songs that most move us, those that inspire and encourage us in the faith, and those that we have learned and wish to pass on to those who come after us. The songs that a community treasures always represent a very loved and appreciated collection. It was the same for the Israelites in Biblical times. That is why the Bible has its own hymn book: the Book of Psalms.

In Hebrew, the book is called *tehillim*, which means "hymns." This condition of poems to be sung is also found in the English name: "psalms," a word that comes from the Latin *psalterium*, a stringed musical instrument, similar to a small harp, which was used in the temple to accompany ritual songs together with other instruments.

The Book of Psalms is a collection of one hundred fifty poems that were sung in the Temple of Jerusalem during religious services, during feasts and at prayer time. The Hebrew text of the Psalms includes marks between the words indicating the musical notes with which they should be sung. To be sure, it is not a pentagram, but rather a series of signs that show the singer the accent and tone in which the verses are to be sung. To this day, when they are read in the synagogues, the melody annotated in the text itself is still followed.

There are some curious facts about the psalms. For example, two psalms are the same (14 and 53) and 70 is repeated in 40:13–18. Or the fact that they are divided into five books, each of which ends with a stanza of praise: 41:14; 72:19; 89:53; 106:48; and Psalm 150, all of which is a song of praise to close the book. This division into five books emulates the five books of the Torah (Pentateuch) and thus presents itself as a mirror of those texts, with the nuance of poetry and the cadence of song.

One characteristic of the psalms in the Bible is that they are texts in which the human voice is heard. Prophets or sages speak as if God were expressing Himself through them. But in the psalms, the voice is that of a human being. It has been said that, while through most of the Bible God's voice "comes down" to humans, in the psalms it is the human voice that "rises" to God. This opinion might be very schematic, and it might distort reality, but, even with limitations, it still expresses a genuine feeling. This is why the psalms penetrate so deeply into those who read them, because they speak as if we ourselves were speaking.

Alberto Ricciardi (1922–1999)

A EUROPEAN UNIVERSITY, OR a center for higher learning would have been honored to receive someone who mastered all the languages around him and countless of dead tongues as well. He would have stood out among his colleagues and occupied the highest positions in view of his knowledge and sagacity in penetrating to the most intricate nooks and crannies of the Scriptures. But although he was born in Italy, the Spirit had prepared him for these southern lands, for the open prairies of the Pampas so that he could be part of this remote area of the globe, and of the Waldensians who proclaim their faith in the resurrected Christ.

He was profoundly humble. He was little given to writing of what he most knew about because he considered that others had already said what he wanted to say or because he thought that his ideas had not yet matured enough to be printed. I suspect that this held something of not wanting to show that he knew too much, that he surpassed us all, and he did not like that. Thus, the writings that he left us are few but acute, worthy of a place in libraries.

He was a specialist in the Ethiopic book of Enoch, a little frequented apocalyptic work, and sometimes even forgotten by most Biblical scholars because it dealt with such a relegated and remote community. However, Enoch belongs to the sacred canon of the Ethiopian Church and, in its pages believers of that other faraway land, find meaning for their lives as they hear the divine Word.

Perhaps, for Alberto, studying a book like Enoch may have been a symbol of his own exile: to his South American destiny he

Alberto Ricciardi (1922–1999)

added the destiny of being a thorough reader of a text born in the remote and dusty horn of Africa.

In God's plan, Alberto Ricciardi occupied a special place. Several generations of pastors know more of the Bible because real learning went on in his classes. So much so, that it was necessary to study beforehand to get the most out of them. He bequeathed us memorable phrases that will remain with those of us who were his students for as long as our memories last; like this which describes him so well: "If you don't know, why do you ask?"; because good questions come from study, not from ignorance. And without meaning to, he bequeathed us—and I am sure he would not like to hear this—the pride of having shared classrooms with one of a kind scholar, one who could have reached the highest academic honors but preferred to stay and talk to us at ground level.

There are those who might think that he seemed wise by contrast with our regions that are little given to knowledge of antiquity and the Orient. I do not think so. In my opinion, what was wise about Alberto went beyond the multiple grammars that populated his personal library and even his knowledge of the Bible. His wisdom—the kind that remains, the kind that is undefeated by death—resided in his fear of God. He would say: "It doesn't matter whether you are a believer or an agnostic, a Christian or of any other faith, the *ruach adonai* (the "breath of God") is in the body of every person and this is why we must be the guardians of our neighbor's life." For Alberto, hurting a human being meant hurting God. Today his remains nourish the land of Uruguay.

The Library

IN THE LIBRARY'S MAGAZINE rack I found the last copy of the *Biblical Archeological Review*. This encounter led me to think about the anxiety in the excavations, about the expectations of coming across the unexpected. That's where my thoughts wandered.

Of the treasures that time and dust doom to be forgotten, some return to history when the archeologist's luck touches them. With rare exceptions, no more than ten percent of the surface of any ancient Biblical city has been excavated. Archeologists know that there is not much margin for error and take great pains in choosing where to sink their shovels. Thus they bring back to life jars, tools, daggers that perhaps plunged into a body; jewels, combs and bronze mirrors that once reflected a face and now are dull; rustic stone knives and oil lamps; bones and coins.

But the greatest luck, the one all yearn for in secret but is only granted to a few, is to find in an ancient city the luminous site of a library. Words and ceramic speak to the archeologist, but texts speak a hundred times more. Because instruments rot but texts do not; as there remain written the things that were wished to preserve, from a harsh order to an intimate letter, from a contract between parties to a fearful prayer to God.

|Every ancient city, however small, had its library. Public documents, orders issued by kings, sacred texts, school manuals, calendars, astrological predictions (the most elaborate science of the time), lists of kings and censuses of plebeians, everything was there; each detail neatly written on tablets of baked clay. Librarians

The Library

had the task of ordering and classifying each item and ensuring that they were available to those who wished to consult them.

In 1887, on the East coast of the Nile, the library of *el-Amarna* was unearthed with letters dated in 1350 B.C. In 1968 it was the library of Mari, that embraces the Euphrates and dates back to 2900 B.C. Between those years, the libraries of Ugarit, of the Assyrians and the Sumerians, and of the Hittites, came back to life. Each people, jealous of their texts, kept them with care, and even with devotion.

Without a doubt, the libraries of today follow the tradition of guarding documents prepared by human beings that the community considers worthy of preservation. They have room for everything: the thesaurus—the code book by which books are classified—is a map of the universe and, when a new galaxy is discovered (that is, when a new discipline of human knowledge with its corresponding new word is created), a space is added and both the universe and the library expand forward.

But libraries also expand backward. When a book that talks about a past that was hitherto unrecorded is incorporated, it extends knowledge in that direction, in what Paul Ricoeur calls the "neo-past." Thus, libraries reproduce the universe on their shelves, challenge us to acknowledge how little we know and—with mercy—offer us their resources to reduce or disguise our ignorance.

A halo of mystery appears upon discovering that libraries feed us back. There is no book, however simple, whose author has not gone to a library to find inspiration for his or her work. Thus, every library contains the germ of its own growth.

Ernesto Sábato once said that in order to write well, it was necessary to read a lot and abstain from writing. Only when the pressure becomes intolerable, should the pen begin to trace words. How can this mandate be carried out without having a library nearby?

I have gone through large and small libraries, and in each one I have discovered something I had not known before. I am grateful to all of them. Sometimes proximity and everydayness make us lose sight of the magnitude of what we have, and the possibility of enjoying the gifts received slips by. The library, my library, is a privileged place in which I sense the continuity of those Oriental libraries.

The Bible and First Things

Who can decipher the origin of something? Theories are exhausted in vain and replaced by others, always novel and challenging. During my first years, I thought that the Bible was the first book, before everything and everyone. Then I learned that when Abraham arrived in Egypt the pyramids were already ancient and had been plundered. However, when I peruse its pages now I perceive in them the flavor of the first things, as if I came near that primitive Adam who named what he discovered in order to incorporate it into the universe (because there is no existence without a name) and inaugurated together with Eve the first love and the first tear. There is a beginning and an end in the Bible and on that path the meaning of life is unfolding. It is a blessing to have received it.

Martha of Bethany, the Invisible

WE HAVE TWO CHARACTERS and two confessions that come together in time. Peter's is multiplied by three in the Gospels and Martha's is only mentioned in the Gospel of John. Peter's occurs under examination by Jesus and Martha's as part of the message that anticipates the resurrection of the dead and of Jesus himself. Peter's is shorter; Martha's includes the affirmation of Jesus as the Messiah. Both are foundational and deserve our admiration.

However, Christian tradition has celebrated Peter's confession and passed over Martha's. This woman is remembered as the one who ran after dust and dishes so her house would shine, not as the only one who forcibly declared the saving identity of Jesus, the one who before her brother Lazarus' tomb confessed her faith in the resurrection that comes through Jesus the Christ. Going through the text allows us to see that her faith and her testimony were not hidden by the account, but rather were diluted in the memory that should call them forth.

Nancy Bedford has pointed out this paradox. She leads us to think about what would have happened if, instead of Jesus calling Peter Satan right after his confession, he had done so to Martha or any other woman. We think that we would have rivers of pages written on the evil that resides in the female flesh; with these words the Lord would have confirmed the suspected perversion that nestles in her curves, from the lust of Eve to the necessity of being a virgin in order to conceive without sin. Peter is forgiven this and much more: his poor weak faith that does not allow him to keep walking on the water; his lack of sagacity in understanding the parables; his triple denial at a crucial moment in the life of Jesus.

Of the many ways about ignoring a reality, making it invisible is the most suited for indifference to eat it away. It is noteworthy that the Bible of Jerusalem, perhaps the most erudite of all the study Bibles, takes up three fourths of a page of notes commenting the passage that contains Peter's declaration of faith (Matthew 16:16) and gives only a few lines to Martha's confession, none of them dedicated to the confession itself (John 11:27). Martha's confession goes unnoticed, as if this confession did not exist; but since it does exist, it is made almost invisible so that a few can see it.

The Junkyard or the Rebirth of the Lost

Rusty and corroded materials appear to reign in this place. Cracks determine that each item is at the end of what were, to differing degrees, glorious days. Some held up prestigious and proud, and others were of humbler origin, but in all cases, they belonged to a place in life that now seems to have vanished away. But this is not so. A deeper look begins to reveal that beneath the dry surfaces, the strength of the iron still wants to vibrate, and some noble wood still wants to rekindle the eyes that behold it.

Objects reach this warehouse defeated, the result of a cold decision to put an end to what was once their place of origin, but they have a calling for life and yearn to return. They resist dying, and this is the place where they will have their chance. An unrepeatable equality takes place here, because the window from the palace lies side by side with the window from the laborer's house; the roof tile that came from France lays next to corrugated iron sheets; sophisticated railings mix with plain ones. From there they will go to different destinations, sometimes similar to the original ones, although a plebeian house may adorn itself with palace castoffs or fashion may transform those cheap old blinds into an expensive prized item to be displayed in a new house of sophisticated design.

The junkyard is like a country doctor's waiting room, where a ranch owner and a farm hand wait together and converse about their aches and pains which turn out to be similar. But after seeing

The Junkyard or the Rebirth of the Lost

the doctor, each one leaves and returns to his own place in the town and in the world.

There are three dimensions to a junkyard: the place itself, the objects it holds, and the reconstruction of the objects. The place looks like a labyrinth of hazardous narrow passages. Each section is characterized for its repetitious pattern, exacerbating the feeling of being lost. Dozens of railings, doors and beams are superimposed in intimidating apparent disarray. How to identify so many objects? How to discover their identity if they all look the same? Here you must discover that only a careful, patient look will allow one piece to be distinguished from another, because ultimately, no two items are alike: in the end we discover that every object has its own name.

The deposited objects call out to those who draw near them. They seem to be clamoring to be chosen and removed from this infamous place into which they have been forced. They are there but they long to get out of the junkyard to come alive again. They are aware that they were not created to lie, nearly dead, far away from people, but to be part of the dynamics of a house or a garden. The window wants someone to look through its panes; the rail calls the hand to lean on it.

The third dimension is the one that gives meaning to all the rest. The objects are there because they have a future and, although they may seem to have died, it is not so. In this dimension, people intervene once more, finding things that will go to new places where they will come back to life. The expected piece is looked for until it is found. It is a contest in which no one loses, because sooner or later all will find their place and their reward.

The rescue process is as follows: first, the eye of the chooser must rest on the object and mark it; next are the hands of the craftsman that will restore it with his acids, brushes and rasps. Although it might seem that the original piece is being rebuilt, in reality nothing will be the same as before. Nuances, thicknesses, lengths and widths will be changed almost in secret, but everything, with its new name, will shine once more like it did on the first day.

The Voice of Antonio Porchia
In memory of Susana Raimondo

IN THE EARLY 20TH century, a young immigrant arrived in Argentina from Italy, fleeing from hunger and death. He settled in a neighborhood in the south of Buenos Aires. Not only did he manage to save his life, but in these lands he found the fertility to develop his thinking. He possessed a rare virtue that allowed him to approach reality, starting at the surface, penetrating it in such a way that shortly after inquiring into it, the weight of the words began to be too much, forcing him to cut them back in order to build phrases that were austere in syllables but dense in meaning. He died full of years and wisdom, and empty of money in a hospital of Buenos Aires. His name was Antonio Porchia and he bequeathed us only one book: enigmatic, profound and beautiful. He called it *Voices*. One of its pages reads:

> And if you reach manhood,
> what else could you reach?

Let us take a moment to savor this thought. Perhaps today the masculine form of the aphorism might grate on us, but such a limitation was no doubt missing from Porchia's feeling. He was speaking to us, men and women radically made of flesh and bone, hurt by the humanity we bear inside, and he faces us with a reality that is both beautiful and brutal: we are who we are.

On the one hand, he speaks of "reaching. . .." You do not arrive at being human; you reach this by a painful road on which you become aware that *existing* is not the same as *being*; also, that it is not enough to breathe and eat for years to fulfill the destiny for which we were created.

Suddenly, we stop to look at a foot, or the strength of an arm, or the speed with which our eyes adjust to a point in space. The feet that take us where we will find what we are searching for. The arm that leads the shovel or drives the hand that wields the pencil that writes that letter we've been putting off. The eyes that look, that guide us and capture a subtle gesture which is imperceptible to others. Reaching *that* means understanding the immensity of human life, that window to the infinite that is the heart that beats and feels.

But this task of knowing ourselves intimately is obstructed by the persistent devaluation to which life is subjected to, its daily depreciation, at times subtle and at times flagrant. Beginning with the economy, when it tells us breezily that there are not too few job openings but too many people; or when VIP rooms, clothes or sectors are advertised for *very important people* only. And we ask ourselves: *who isn't important?* Being human is making a commitment to that which we are and for which we were created, and to proclaim the intrinsic value of life, all life.

(From Antonio Porchia, *Voces*)

Jorge Luis Borges and the Infamous Preacher

IN *A UNIVERSAL HISTORY of Infamy*, Borges describes the lives of crooks and imposters. Among all these cretins we find the adventures of Lazarus Morell, who in the early 19th century had set up an ingenious slave business. First, he helped them escape from their masters, promising to take them to a state where slavery had been abolished. After they escaped, he recaptured them and sold them to a new master in another slave state and so on until he got rid of the poor unfortunate people by killing them.

Before arriving at that occupation, this enterprising man from the southern United States had undertaken other forms of criminal activity, one of which was being an itinerant preacher who made tears and conversions spring forth from those who heard him speak from the pulpit. His preaching was as impeccable as it was false. This is his story, as penned by Borges:

> He was not ignorant of the Scriptures, and he preached with singular conviction. "I once saw Lazarus Morell in the pulpit," wrote the owner of a gambling house in Baton Rouge, "and I heard his edifying words and saw the tears come to his eyes. I knew he was a fornicator, a nigger-stealer, and a murderer in the sight of the Lord, but tears came to my eyes too."
>
> Another testimony to those holy outpourings is provided by Morell himself: "I opened the Bible at random, put my finger on the first verse that came to hand—St. Paul it was—and preached for an hour and twenty

minutes. Crenshaw and the boys didn't put that time to bad use, neither, for they rounded up all the folks' horses and made off with 'em. We sold 'em in the state of Arkansas, all but one bay stallion, the most spirited thing you ever laid eyes on, that I kept for myself. . .

Pulpit infamy is not a monopoly of this fictional character, for it also happens in our day. Those who profit from the faith of believers and those who with no fear and trembling put the Bible at the service of their niggardly personal interests, would make a long list starting from vile businesses to manipulating the offerings that are given with reverence and candor by the parishioners.

We are far removed from the times in which it was thought that a consuming fire would fall on those who distorted sacred things. The sons of Aaron died for a fault of this kind (Leviticus 10:1–2); Ananias and Sapphira suffered the same fate (Acts 5:1–10). Perhaps we would feel some satisfaction if it were so, but few today fear such punishment for deceiving their neighbors.

Evangelina Rodríguez

Pastor Teresa Solíz told me the following story.

Evangelina had given birth by cesarean section and was ordered bed rest. She lived in the Budge District, in southern Greater Buenos Aires, where it flooded when it rained long. On the second day of her convalescence, it began to rain, and the waters rose. Her two-year-old son was home alone and, when the rising water gathered strength, it began to sweep away everything on its path. The water that took furniture and garbage, also took the body of her child, and with it, also his life.

Evangelina went looking for him downstream, where everything that gets dragged builds up, but she could not find the child's body. She searched through the mud for two days on both sides of the stream, and among the filthy remains left behind by the current. The body was not recovered and the little angel slept forever with no wake and not even a fistful of earth to cover him, nor a gravestone to remember him.

While searching for her son in the most insanitary places, Evangelina contracted an abdominal infection, forcing her to fight for her life for several days. Her body finally overcame death, and she was able to move forward.

After these events, and throughout her lifetime, Evangelina knitted and put together quilts of multicolored squares that she herself designed. And while she knitted, she thought. As the yarn ran through her hands, she meditated. At night she also meditated. She knit and held her thoughts close to her heart.

Evangelina Rodríguez

Evangelina is known in the neighborhood as the Methodist lady who went to funerals and prayed for the life of the deceased. She arrived and prayed, talked to the family and consoled them. She gave a word of encouragement to those who found no consolation; she calmed the desperate with words of faith. Evangelina mourned a neighbor, a grandfather, a young mother who left little ones behind; but in secret, throughout her lifetime, she mourned for her little angel who had had no funeral.

William C. Morris, Living at Dawn

HIS FATHER SOUGHT IN these lands the prosperity denied to him in his native England. Thus he arrived in a colony in Paraguay; from there he moved to Santa Fe and from there to the La Boca district in Buenos Aires. His mother had died before they left for South America. William read a lot but had to work to help feed his two brothers, his sister and his father. He was barely able to go to school. William's childhood was very hard and arduous.

Some prefer to forget the bad times, others remember them to bear in mind that others are suffering the same fate right now. The latter leads some to despair and anguish, and others are led to fight more strongly so that this tragedy does not overshadow the life of new persons. William Morris was one of the latter ones: he saw in each poor boy and girl a mirror of his own poverty and knew by experience how hard it would be for them to face life with hope. His Christian faith moved him to join them and do everything in his power to offer them tools to reach what society and destiny were keeping them from.

There are landscapes and geographies that model people. In that neighborhood, perhaps because of the teeming nature of the city, hitherto unknown to him, he perceived the wretched end of so many children unless they were offered education, values to live by and inspiring life models.

He knew the whirlwind of a life that grows without horizons and is dragged toward the worst and wander aimlessly. But he did not deceive himself with glib formulas. The name of the home and the school he founded was no coincidence: The Dawn. Dawn is the time when night yields and reality begins to change. There are small rays of light, an awakening of the sky, a call to get ready for what is coming. He conceived his task as that of preparing the children to face life with all its challenges and beauty, its violence and friendship. He worked for them to acquire strength of body and spirit with which to overcome the injustice of a hostile society.

He was an Anglican pastor, although he had participated in the Methodist Church in La Boca. His remains returned to Sohan, England, where he had been born sixty-eight years before, and there they rest from so much knocking at doors with his eternal briefcase. On his tombstone it says: "The path of the righteous is like the light of dawn, which shines brighter and brighter until full day." His life was a permanent dawn, walking toward the light until its brightness illuminated everything.

The Armenian Alphabet

I HAD THE PLEASURE of walking through the streets of Yerevan, capital of Armenia. The writing on the walls strikes the eyes of those who must admit their illiteracy in a city that breathes several thousand years of culture.

It was Eric Gill, the great British typesetter, who said that letters are things, not drawings of things, but he gave them esthetic rather than ontological value. So he decided to adorn texts with his harmonious, clear, soft letters. This is how I see Armenian.

Armenia is a nation that has changed geographies several times in its history, always yielding territory. A country harassed by great powers that have taken advantage of its lands and its young people. Around 1915, when the eyes of the world were set on the events taking place in the fields of Europe, while everyone was looking that way, one-and-a-half million Armenians were being exterminated, and their land was snatched away. Hunger, cold and munitions put an end to those unique and unrepeatable lives.

If you look west you can see Mount Ararat, the majestic legendary peak that is in the soul of these people, where Scripture locates the descent of the ark built by Noah to rescue life after the Flood. Like all symbols, rather than a snowy mountain, it is a way of being, a witness of that which endures beyond violence and humiliation.

The Armenians are the only people I know who celebrate the creation of their alphabet; they have a date and each year it is remembered as a magnificent day. Mesrob Mashtots created

The Armenian Alphabet

the alphabet in the year 406 A.D. and his figure is exalted beyond that of generals and kings, revealing that here letters are more prestigious than swords and crowns. He took the shapes from the Greek and other alphabets, and recreated the letters with their own profiles that represented the sounds of his language. With them, soon after, the Bible was translated into Armenian, which not only consolidated the language and its new writing, but also gave its people identity.

Historians state that Mashtots invented the alphabet. However, the Armenians say its origin is divine and that the thirty-six letters were given by God through his hands. I suspect that this is true.

Martin Luther

As A YOUNG MAN he worried about finding the path that would save his life. He was not convinced by the usual methods of penance, confession, harsh flagellation and fasting. He practiced them with fruition in his monastery, but perceived that there was something else in the Gospels that he could not yet make out. He studied the Scriptures in their original languages—Hebrew and Greek—and went through the philosophy and theology of his day. Soon he was a doctor and a professor, and he was assigned the Bible Reading chair at the University of Wittemberg, where he taught dozens of students. In those classes he understood that the key to finding what he was seeking was in a renewed reading of the Bible.

After some time, he made Christian faith mature with three affirmations that still dazzle us to this day: he pointed out that the key to salvation lies in faith alone, in grace alone and in Scripture alone. These ideas, which simply stated seem harmless, impacted on the heart of a stagnant theology that prevented believers from valuing their own consciences and referred them to the guardianship of the church for every relevant detail of their lives.

Luther's thinking makes it clear that human beings have been created in a relationship with God, and that they have been given tools to communicate with the Creator directly. God is who approaches human beings to redeem them, and not persons who reach Him by merit and actions. In that act of approaching voluntarily, God freely offers His love and grace to save their lives.

Martin Luther

We owe Martin Luther for rescuing the Bible as a book for everyone, consolidating the tongue that became that of Goethe, renewing the art of translation, public education, the Reformation and the Counterreformation, the academic vocation of going to the sources, the exaltation of preaching, the value of one's own conscience, the church as a community of believers, the suspicion that things might be different from what they seem (followed by Galileo, Darwin, Freud, etc.), the one hundred and one volumes of the Weimar edition, the novel Moby Dick which is a metaphor of evil, Bach's Mass in B Minor, and a new dimension of the word grace. Together with this, and much more, is Thesis 62 of the 95 Theses: "The true treasure of the Church is the Most Holy Gospel of the glory and the grace of God."

There is a story—or a legend, it doesn't matter which—that says that it was a lightning bolt that fell near him and endangered his life that led him to become a monk and study theology. Perhaps we owe this revolution in the Christian faith to a conjunction of storm clouds and a spark. It would be one more proof that the ways of the Lord are unpredictable.

Far Away and Long Ago

It is common for time to pass and to go forgetting minor details even about things that struck us at a given time. On other occasions, we forget the big things and only the little ones remain. I wish to share a paragraph, just a few lines that I have not forgotten, which I believe will never be erased or will be so when everything else is erased.

The book is a classic, and as such, many know of it but few have read it. It's a shame. Approach its pages without haste, without looking for stridence, and you will find the reality of life on the great green plains seen through the eyes of a child who grows vigorous and takes in everything with fascination and wonder. What is striking in *Far Away and Long Ago* is the sensitivity in the contemplation of a carrion hawk, a huge hare, the blood on the grass after the beheading of a soldier, the woman who begs for the levy not take her son, a knocked-down nest, the stream and the flamencos, the knife fight and the fear that war will reach home.

I am interested in sharing a paragraph that needs a few introductory words. Hudson tells us that they frequently received visitors at night in their home. Persons, most often strangers, who were on their way south or north to Buenos Aires, who knocked at their door and asked to be taken in for the night.

He tells us that his parents always received those who were passing by, regardless of who they were. He tells us that there were persons of all types, some of them very simple, with rustic table manners and speech. This made William and his siblings laugh, sometimes openly. The next paragraph recounts the words of his mother and reveals the reason for being hospitable in the solitude of the pampas. Hudson writes:

> And she would sometimes say to us afterwards that she could not laugh with us because she remembered the poor fellow probably had a mother somewhere in a distant country who was perhaps thinking on him at the very time he was at the table with us, and hoping and praying that in his wanderings he would meet with some who would be kind to him.
>
> (From William E. Hudson, *Far Away and Long Ago*, XXIV)

Authors

IN THE 4TH CENTURY Ambrose of Milan wrote *Veni Redentor Gentium*; in Mexico, Vicente Mendoza wrote *I have a friend, Christ the Lord*; Juanita de Balloch wrote *To you omnipotent Lord God*; Fanny Crosby wrote *Jesus is tenderly calling*; in 1902, after hearing an elderly woman pray beside her, Adelaide Pollard wrote *Have thine own way, Lord, thou art the potter, I am the clay*; Emily Elliott wrote *Thou didst leave thy throne and thy kingly crown when thou camest to earth for me*; Francis of Assisi wrote *All creatures of our God and King lift up your voice and with us sing*; John of Damascus wrote *Come, you faithful, raise the strain of triumphant gladness*; Mary Lathbury wrote *Break thou the bread of life, dear Lord, to me, as thou didst break the loaves beside the sea*.

Alberto López wrote *Give us, Lord, your bread this day*; Henri Abraham César Malan, who was forbidden to preach in Geneva in 1817, wrote *What is the star that brightly shines new radiance from the East?*; Nicolás Martínez wrote *Christ lives, tears be gone*; Aurelius Clemens Prudentius, Fourth Century poet and politician, wrote *Fruit of divine love, genesis of creation*; Isabel de Rodríguez wrote *Loving Father, I have sinned and fallen into temptation*; in the Eighteenth Century Charles Wesley wrote *Love divine, all loves excelling*; Joseph Brigg wrote *Jesus! and shall it ever be a mortal man ashamed of thee?*, and it was Febe's favorite hymn; in Brazil, Sime Monteiro wrote *I sing a new song in the world*; Pablo Sosa wrote *May this church be a tree, at the back of your house, may there be rejoicing and prayer beneath its branches*.

Authors

In the immensity of Canada, weak and ill, Civilla D. Martin wrote *Be not dismayed whate'er betide, God will take care of you; beneath his wings of love abide, God will take care of you*; someone whose name we do not know wrote in Latin *"O come all ye faithful, joyful and triumphant, o come ye, o come ye to Bethlehem*; in the Fifteenth Century, Daniel Ben Judah wrote what the Sephardic Jews recite at the closing of Shabat, *the God of Abraham, Sing praises to his name; who was, and is, and is to be, and still the same!*; in Switzerland Anders Frostenson wrote *Many are the light beams from the one light; our one light is Jesus*; in the United States Anna Bartlett Warner wrote *Jesus loves me; this I know for the Bible tells me so*; in 1974 young people at a camp wrote *Like you, Lord, like you love us, we want to love.*

In Cameroon, Abel Kuinji wrote *Everything is done for the glory of God, as long as we are guided by His love*; Juan Gattinoni wrote *So you will always be among us, for you to join us in communion*; Ylva Eggerhon wrote *Do not fear, there is a secret sign, a name that shelters you wherever you go*; in his home in Banfield, Alberto Giacumbo wrote *Jesus is there, Jesus is talking there*; in Bolivia and in his native aymara tongue, Zoilo Yanapa wrote *Tatanaka, mamanaca, sarantañani*; Effie Wright Chastain, who was born in Mexico but was a missionary in Cuba, wrote *In the silence of the dark, the king's birth proclaim*; in Uruguayan lands Alba and Mabel Colombo wrote *Let us share together the divine light that brought the baby Jesus to the world*; in the 16th century Venantiuis Fortunatus wrote *Welcome, happy morning, age to age shall say; hell today is vanquished, heaven is won today.*

Then came melodies, songs, time.

Uriah, the Murdered Prophet

MARTYRDOM IS NOT USUAL among Biblical prophets if we go by the information from its pages. But we would like to mention a case that recalls so many Jewish and Christian martyrs of the faith throughout history and, closer to us, our own Latin America. We are referring to the prophet Uriah, son of Shamaiah, whose story is told in Jeremiah 26:20–23. This is the dark tale:

There was another man who prophesied in the name of the Lord, Uriah the son of Shemaiah from Kiriath-jerarim. He prophesied against this city and against this land in words like those of Jeremiah. And when King Jehoiakim, with all his warriors and all the princes, heard his words, the king sought to put him to death; but when Uriah heard of it, he was afraid and fled and escaped to Egypt. Then King Jehoiakim sent to Egypt certain men, Elnathan the son of Acbor and others with him, and they fetched Uriah from Egypt and brought him to King Jehoiakim, who slew him with the sword and cast his dead body into the burial place of the common people.

Uriah was a disciple of Jeremiah and preached that God did not approve of the injustices and idolatry practiced in the royal palace. The king lost no time in defending his privileges and those of his entourage, and gave the order to capture and kill the prophet. Uriah found out and fled to Egypt.

At that time, Egypt was a place very far away from Canaan and it took several days to go through the desert and reach the delta of the Nile. For Uriah, Egypt was a place of safe asylum, far from danger, as it had been for others before him, and would be for Jesus and his family several centuries later (Matthew 2:13–15).

We do not know his mother's name but we do know his father's. We can imagine Shemaiah's sadness on knowing the fate of his son, the same one that had filled him with pride because the Lord had called him to the ministry of His prophets. Let us think about his mother, asking God to help her son in exile, to find someone on the road who would receive him and treat him kindly to assuage his loneliness. Even in the midst of her pain she would trust that distance would protect his life.

But the king sent a retinue to Egypt to capture him and take him back to be murdered before him and his body thrown into a nameless tomb. As we have experienced on many occasions in our countries, the complicity of the powerful has no national borders, is not detained by Customs and does not require scrupulous documents to be pored over by Immigration.

Nelson Mandela

Those who knew him say that integrity was his main trait. Twenty-seven years in prison were unable to bow his spirit, his ideas or his will. He once said: ". . . It will forever remain an indelible blight on human history that apartheid crime ever occurred."

Apartheid means "separation" in Afrikaans, a tongue in which German and Dutch meet, and it is only spoken in South Africa and Namibia. As a political system, it refers to a series of laws created by the white South African government between the years 1947 and 1953 that were in force until 1992. They established the physical separation of Whites and Blacks; they created a record of persons dividing them by races; provinces were created for Blacks.

Ultimately, their objective was to prevent Black majorities from voting in South Africa and obtaining political control of the country. But the laws not only established that people of color—as opposed to those of another color, white—did not have the right to vote, but also regulated the places where they could live, the schools they could attend, the hospitals where they could be treated, the beaches where they could bathe and the parks where the children were allowed to play. The apartheid laws prohibited marriage between persons of different color and penalized with prison time sexual relations between people of different colored skin. In some public places, access was denied to Blacks and dogs; in others, dogs were allowed.

Nelson Mandela opposed all of that. He was a lawyer and knew the laws but, more than that, he was a believer and trusted that God was on the side of the marginalized and humiliated. He knew that faith could sustain the spirit in the worst times, and with it he faced his struggle and his dreams.

When he was freed from prison, he was elected President of his country in the first free elections when Black citizens were allowed vote in the entire history of South Africa. It was in 1994 and, where from that place, he contributed to organizing a nation without racism, with real democracy and with equal justice for all, even in the midst of the nation's difficult general conditions.

One of his noblest acts was to establish the *Truth and Reconciliation Commission*. It was a mediating organ where the victims of human rights violations could submit their cases and where those who had assaulted them could confess their crime and ask the victims for forgiveness. Forgiveness was in the hands of the victims; if they forgave, they went free. The chairman he designated for this commission was Anglican Archbishop Desmond Tutu, who coined the phrase, "Without forgiveness there is no future, but without confession there can be no forgiveness."

All languages are legitimate, beautiful and worthy of honor, because people communicate with them. It has been rightly said that even the smallest and most obscure language has all the necessary conditions for an Alfonsina Storni to rise up and make it shine. It is sad that the only word we recognize from the Afrikaans language is *apartheid*.

Stephen or the Hurricane of Words

IT WAS NECESSARY TO find people to take care of the daily tasks, because the disciples were busy praying and teaching. We see that the Church was still being formed and already there were problems among the members: the Greek believers complained that the Jewish believers discriminated against them. To ease tensions and balance out the loads, they chose seven persons: Stephen, Phillip, Prochorus, Nicanor, Timon, Parmenas and Nicolaus. They are all Greek names, which indicate that their complaints were heard. We know little about them, except for Stephen and Phillip the Evangelist; perhaps they carried out their ministry smoothly, attending to the needs of the widows and the poor. But this mission cost Stephen his life.

From the known accounts, more than serving the tables, Stephen preached the good news of Jesus. Given his status as a Jerusalem resident of Hellenic culture, he probably irritated the Jews of the Diaspora more than the natives. In fact, the ones who asked for his capture were Alexandrian Jews, from Cyrene and Asia. They bribed and lied and managed to get him taken before the Sanhedrin and the High Priest, accused of perverting the faith of Israel.

Sometimes a question is taken by the wind; at others it unleashes a hurricane. "Is this so?" He probably thought that the question would decompress the tension; that this young man would seek to calm things down and get on with his life, keeping his ideas to himself or sharing them in the intimacy of this new community of Jews who maintained that the Nazarene crucified on the last Passover had resurrected and would return to judge the Earth. It was not the first time that craziness of this type had appeared and vanished after a while. It is very probable, extremely probable, that the High Priest wanted to hear from Stephen's mouth, words of apology and repentance, and thus everyone would go home satisfied and in peace.

But Stephen unleashed the hurricane of the Gospel. He could have kept silent or retracted, but he decided to be faithful to the word he had received. First, he called them brothers and fathers, and next he reminded them of the history of the acts of God in favor of His people Israel from Abraham to Solomon. Then he confronted them with their rejection of the prophets, with their attitude of not hearing what God had to say. He said the harshest thing: "You always resist the Holy Spirit."

Stephen preached with energy and knowledge, but in this case there was no conversion. Ire rose against him; he was dragged out of the city and murdered by having stones cast at him. In his agony, he pleaded for the forgiveness of his murderers.

That the name Stephen (in Greek *Stephanos*) means "crown" adds to his glory. He received a crown that no king had ever received before or will receive forever after.

(Acts 6—7)

Of the Origin of Chapters and Verses

THE MOST ANCIENT TEXTS we have of both the Old and the New Testaments are not divided into chapters and verses. What's more, the words are not even separated in the New Testament, since in Greek it was not customary to divide them but to write in continuous text. This made them hard to read for those who were not specialized in the Biblical languages, and even for those who were.

The first to try to make reading easier were rabbis during the 7th to 10th centuries. Among the many data they added to the text in the margins, they also introduced a division of the texts according to subjects and stopping places, but they did not number them. This was done for use in liturgy and special prayers. Judaism still uses this division today in its editions of the Old Testament.

In Christian circles, it was not until the 12th century that Stephen Langton, who was the Archbishop of Canterbury, introduced the division of the entire Bible into chapters. He did it in the Latin Vulgate Bible, and it is the division that we find in our modern present day Bibles.

Time passes and we arrive at the 16th century, when a French printer divided the text into verses. His name was Robert Estienne and he was born in Paris but ended his days in Geneva, protected by the church of that city. It is said that he divided the New Testament while he rode from Paris to Lyon on horseback, but that is probably a legend. We are not even sure that Estienne saw the edition with verses, for he died in 1559.

Of the Origin of Chapters and Verses

As far as we know, it was in 1560 that a group of English exiles who had taken refuge in Geneva worked on editing the Bible in a language that would be edifying, facilitate reading and have tools to understand it. That is how the so-called *Geneva Bible* came into being and became very popular in England and Scotland, until it was replaced by the King James Version beginning in 1604. This Geneva Bible was the first to include the division into chapters and verses that Langton and Estienne had established and that we now use in our modern Bibles.

Don José and Doña Josefa

HE DISEMBARKED IN THE port of Buenos Aires from Barcelona around 1910. He was from Badalona, in Cataluña, and his parents had sent him far away to protect him from a possible new Carlist war. He was fifteen years old when he arrived in a city that was preparing to celebrate its Centennial and receiving thousands of immigrants like him. We know little of his first steps as an independent teenager: he ambled through the city, perhaps meeting other Catalans, and entered a Methodist church. He was a cobbler by trade and practiced it in Chivilcoy and later in Junín. Shortly afterward he prepared to be a pastor. In the Seminary, José Andiñach met Josefa Castro.

Josefa Castro had arrived at around the same time with her parents and siblings, and settled in a cattle ranch in General Madariaga. Her father was the foreman and her brother was a ranch hand there. Later Josefa went to work at the home of some English Methodists in Lomas de Zamora, where she discovered the Evangelical faith. Within a short time she began working as a cook and living at the seminary in Buenos Aires. There she met José. She lost all contact with her family and was not to see her brother Manuel until sixty years later, on an unforgettable afternoon that is still printed on retina and memory.

José and Josefa began their course as preachers of the Gospel in Ramallo, in the year 1920. They continued in Arroyo Seco, then in General Alvear, and from there they went on to San Juan.

Don José and Doña Josefa

While they were in San Juan, on January 15, 1944, the earth trembled, destroying the city in seconds and reducing the temple and parsonage to rubble. Josefa was with their two daughters and four sons, and all survived. José was in Buenos Aires and it was several days before he had word of his family's fate.

From San Juan they went to Villa Mercedes, to finish up their pastorate in Urdinarrain in 1948. Retired, they returned to Villa Mercedes and, from there, first he and then Josefa were to leave forever to rest in the Lord from all their comings and goings. The serene earth of the Andean foothills received them and there still lay their remains.

Their days were many and blessed. They had children and grandchildren. These are the names of the sons and daughters that were born to them and their descendants: Ester, Elena, Esteban, Elías, Eliseo and Ezequiel. Ester married Carlos Ward and had Susana, Dorcas and David. Elena married Américo and had Jorge and Gladis. Esteban married Nilda Muhape and had Pablo, Miriam and Marcelo. Elías married Hilda and had Cachito, who died when he was two, and César. Eliseo married Margarita and had Viviana. Ezequiel married Teresita and had Guido, Maricel, Ana, Jorge, Guadalupe and Silvina.

Adán Buenosayres, Thoughts on Graves

FRIENDS ARE LOST OVER the years, friends with whom distance or ideas created barriers, wore down words and made us lose the pleasure of getting together. But for others it will take death to break the connection. That is why now and again we go to the cemetery to leave the remains of a loved one, a friend, one of those people who, when they part, leave us with a feeling that the world is not whole without them.

Walking among the tall fine trees of the cemetery, I thought what I had already thought many times before. That everything that is good, that is sincere, where we put our heart, is not lost but will be preserved. In some way that we do not understand, the voices—your voice, the voices of those you loved—will return on some faraway day to speak the best words they spoke, the ones you said and were said to you. That is why I look at the graves, most of them with strange names that I read and find beautiful, and I feel an intimate certainty that they are all right, that they are being cared for. I recall a paragraph from that unforgettable novel:

> ... six of us entered the Western Cemetery, bearing a coffin of modest design (four fragile little planks), so light that it seems to carry within not the spent flesh of a dead man but rather the subtle stuff of a concluded poem.
>
> (From Leopoldo Marechal, *Adán Buenosayres*)

Cain and Abel

WHO IS CAIN AND who is Abel? Cain is the elder, the farmer. Abel is the younger one and raises cattle. The former, simply by being first, will receive honor and inheritance. The latter must serve at his brother's farm, because that is what law and custom require. Abel means vapor, lightness, inexistence. Cain means blacksmith or lance, and evokes the hardness of metal. Their names announce their destinies.

Being on the side of the weak does not necessarily mean rejecting the strong. But Cain did not understand that and became angry when he saw that God was pleased with the offering of his weak brother and passed over his own. He did not think about all that he had received; he forgot his privileges and was bitter because for once the honor was for his brother.

The story is well known and I will not tell it here. Cain kills his brother and thereby inaugurates fratricide in human history. He is an archetype and, like them all, he is a symbol of all humankind.

There are two conclusions to be reached, both horrifying. The first is that whenever a person is killed, life is being taken from a brother or a sister. It does not matter if they are adversaries, enemies or guilty of some crime. The blood that is spilled and the lifeless body always belong to the brother or sister with whom we learned our first childhood steps and words.

The second is that fratricide is also deicide. Hurting someone's body to death is destroying the image of God it bears. When violence takes lives, there is less God on Earth.

(From Genesis 4:1–10)

Juana Manso, the Feminist Teacher

HER FATHER SUPPORTED THE May Revolution and became a hero in the wars for independence. When he returned from war, he founded two schools in Buenos Aires. Juana was born from the marriage of José María Manso and Teodora Cuenca, in 1819. A few years later the family moved to Montevideo. While that city was under siege by Manuel Oribe, Juana and her family migrated to Brazil. There Juana married a musician and had two daughters. They returned first to Montevideo and, around 1853, back to Buenos Aires. There her husband abandoned her and left her alone with her two daughters. She was thirty-three years old the day that she decided that she had found the place to carry out her task.

At that time she joined the Methodist Church which, in spite of still using the English language in the congregations (a condition imposed by the government of Rosas), was attempting to blend in, a process that culminated in the beginning of the Spanish-language work in 1867. Juana lent her home for meetings of the small church—we know for a fact that a wedding took place in her house, but it is probable that many other meetings took place there as well.

She has rightly been called the first feminist of Argentina. During her life she dedicated herself to dignifying women and demanding the acknowledgment and respect due to them. She wrote things like the following:

Juana Manso, the Feminist Teacher

> All of my efforts will be devoted to enlightening my [female] compatriots, and they will tend to a single purpose: to emancipate them from the dull old occupations that prevented them until now from using their intelligence, alienating their liberty and even their conscience, to arbitrary authorities opposed to the very nature of things. I wish to, and will, prove that woman's intelligence, far from being an absurdity or a defect, a crime or a folly, is her best adornment, the true source of her virtue and domestic happiness, because God is not contradictory in His works, and when He made the human soul, He did not give it gender.

She was a poet, playwright, journalist, novelist and translator. She founded schools and wrote books to train teachers. With Eduarda Mansilla, she edited the women's magazine *Flor del Aire*, in which she defended the rights of women and demanded that they be given spaces in society. President Sarmiento, with whom she collaborated in her educational task and in the foundation of thirty-four public schools and libraries, used to say to her scornfully when she contradicted him in a conversation: "How dare you!" Because Juana was a woman who dared.

She died at fifty-five years of age, in 1875. Before the pastor paid his last respects, Juana

Juana Manuela Gorriti spoke and said, "Without her we would be submissive, illiterate, held back, ignored. . . ."

Julie Adelaide Hope, a teacher in Paraná

JULIE HOPE AND GEORGE Stearns had arrived in Paraná from the United States, to work as school teachers. They were both part of the first group of teacher trainers that president Sarmiento contracted to form the first official teachers of the country. George Stearns was 23 years old and a graduate from Harvard University. He was the first headmaster of the Normal High School of the city; Julie was a school teacher. She had had her first child at the age of 20, a mentally impaired son born in Boston, who travelled with them to our land. At the age of 22 she had her second son in our country. Three months later, Julie died of tyfhoid fever. It was February of 1872. Alice Houston Luiggi, a descendant of one of the teachers, narrates in her memoirs the events that take place at the time of Julie´s death, which were published later in 1959 under the title: *65 Valiants.*

> "As it seems, Mrs. Stearns was the first Protestant person to die in Paraná, and while the authorities debated as to where this outcast should be buried, her grieving husband remained sitting on her casket, outside the cemetery, throughout three torrid days with its corresponding nights, holding a gun with each hand in order to protect the body from the dangerous wild cats that roamed in the woods at the bank of the river, attracted by the smell of dead flesh. At last came the authorization from the authorities to bury the body near the walls of the sacred cemetery, but from the outside of the boundaries.

Julie Adelaide Hope, a teacher in Paraná

Not much time passed until her sick son followed his mother's footsteps. The only trace that remains of the place where they were buried, is a picture made by her husband."

Stearns' picture which mentions Luiggi, shows the cemetery and the tomb next to the outside wall, because according to the local priest, the cemetery only belonged to Catholics. The negotiations between local authorities and the church authorities had delayed the burial of the body, and the latter authorities prevented a Protestant body to be buried in a place that had been blessed as a Catholic final resting place. A few days later, the boy born in Boston was not able to survive without his mother, and was buried next to her. But Julie's was not the only case. Six years later, Edward Young Haslam, Jorge Luis Borges' great grand-father, teacher and journalist of the Protestant faith, also died in Paraná; and he was also buried on the outside of the cemetery, perhaps close to Julie and her son.

George Stearns left Paraná in 1875 to inaugurate the Normal High School of Tucumán. He complied with his duties, but his sadness knew no end. After a few months in Tucumán, overcome with sorrow, he returned with his young son to his country. Today there's a plaque in the cemetery of Paraná that remembers Julie, the teacher victim of the tyfhoid fever, and of human foolishness.

Dirk Henry Kloosterman

IT IS HARD TO be honest in times of peace. It was a hundred times harder to be so in the vortex in the Argentina of the 1960s and 1970s. If in civilized politics spaces are won and lost in the ballot boxes, at that time there were those who planned to take power by killing their opponents. Thus they installed a culture of death, where the life of the other was worthless and eliminating those who thought differently became normal. And that sick culture first took hundreds and then thousands of men and women whose lives were cut off, and left sons, daughters, wives, mothers and fathers in dark loneliness.

Dirk Henry Kloosterman was a victim of that base hatred. From a young age he understood that he had to be on the side of those who risk the strength of their work to produce wealth. Because what they do moves the world, and without workers there is no social fabric. He understood that they had to join together to defend their rights from the rapacity of capitalism. Thus began his union activity in SMATA, the mechanics' syndicate, which after a long internal career chose him as its General Secretary. From there he worked to build a society with more justice and solidarity.

His union brothers tell that Dirk went off to pray when an important decision had to be made regarding union management. He had learned that evangelical faith leads us to our neighbors and our neighbors are those actual people in front of us. To him, they were his factory coworkers, the plant workers and all those who through their daily efforts and honesty, worked to earn their bread.

Dirk Henry Kloosterman

The Methodist congregation of La Plata counted him among its active members and stood by him until his last day. That was May 22, 1973 and the place was 51st Street, number 1617. When he left in his car, with no guards and completely defenseless, he was murdered in the street by a couple of people who then fled.

We believe that he was not aware of these words that John Chrysostom preached in the 4th century, but we think that Dirk would have appreciated them. John Chrysostom asked his parishioners from the pulpit:

> "If all the rich of a city are put on one side and all the workers on the other, and an unsurmountable wall is built between them so that each community must make do with its own means, which of the two communities do you think will survive?"

Dirk would not hesitate to answer.

(From John Chrysostom,
Homily 34, item 5 on 1 Corinthians)

The Bandoneon, Birth and Destiny

THIS STORY APPEARS TO affirm God's good sense of humor and the labyrinthine nature of his ways. We know that in around 1830 Karl Uhlig modified an English concertina and created an instrument with lighter and nimbler bellows. He presented it at the Leipzig fair but it went unnoticed and few took note of its somewhat annoying sound. We also know that, in mid 19th century Germany, there was renewed religious fervor and a luthier named Heinrich Band sought to create an instrument that would allow church music to be played in remote places and in temples where there was no adequate instrument. He remembered Uhlig's concertina, modified it and added a cord for hanging it from the neck and making it portable. He baptized it with a derivative of his own name (in German *Band*onion) and began to manufacture it.

The instrument was practical for evangelizing in street corners, and playing at funerals and Sunday worship meetings. It spread, always within a limited circuit, as a substitute for greater instruments, like the organ or harmonium. It recalled their sounds and to a certain extent imitated them, but had no voice of its own.

It is now necessary to cross the Atlantic and situate ourselves in Buenos Aires. Around 1870 this city began to receive thousands of immigrants and to see its port and international trade activity grow. The exchange was of grain, meat and cloth, but also of persons and dreams, and with them their soul, their passions, their loneliness and their nostalgia. One of them also took the first bandoneon that disembarked at the port.

It is marvelous to see the twists of history, how destinies cross each other, and how unexpected doors open. In Buenos Aires there were no churches that accepted the bandoneon or any tradition of melodies that yearned for wind and reeds for their execution. But there were dance halls where men and women got together for entertainment after a long day's work.

By the end of the 19th century, those dark port meeting halls gathered Poles, Italians, Russians, newly arrived Spaniards, Germans, Greeks, Arabs, Mulattoes and Turks. In the midst of that confusion of tongues and flavors, they perceived that the melancholy sound of the bandoneon brought them together. Its box and its notes were as foreign to these lands as they all were, but perhaps because of that they felt it increasingly their own. In Buenos Aires, the bandoneon did not belong to anyone; that is why it belonged to everyone. Like these men and women on the banks of the River Plate, it was an orphan; like it, they had no history or lost it or wished to lose it.

We have already said that paradox is on the list of the humorous acts of God. The instrument that was born in Germany for the orderly liturgy of the churches; found its destiny, its splendor and its voice, in the dark low places of Buenos Aires that gave birth to the tango.

The Islam

THE WORD *ISLAM* MEANS "to submit." The Koran indicates that the submission is to God, and Sura 3:18 says: "...there is no god except He, the worshipful, the Ever-Mighty, the Ever-Wise."

Islam was founded by Mohammed in the year 622. That is the year of the migration of Mohammed and his followers from the city of Mecca to Medina, where he organized those who heard him. This event is known as the Hegira (migration) and is considered the beginning of Islam. The Islamic calendar establishes the year one of its era at that time.

Its inspired book is the *Al Quran* or Koran. Tradition says that its pages were given to Mohammed by the Angel Gabriel. Although its texts mention some characters from Judaism and Christianity, the narrations are different from those in the Bible. It is a version of its own and has little to do with the Bible stories. However, those mentions of Abraham, Ishmael, Jesus and others contribute to establishing the brotherhood between the peoples, for Islam recognizes common ancestors in these persons. In the Biblical genealogy, Islam identifies with the lineage of Ishmael.

Islam has three holy places: the cities of Mecca and Medina, both in present-day Saudi Arabia, and the El Aksa mosque, which is located in Jerusalem. Mohammed was born in Mecca and died and was buried in Medina. It is said that, from El Aksa, Mohammed ascended on a nocturnal voyage to heaven. There he met several Biblical characters and then received from God the gift of prayer and prophecy. According to its doctrine, the Biblical teachings of

Abraham, Moses and Jesus are no different in essence from those revealed to Mohammed, but he, by being the last to receive them, transmits them in their most perfect form.

Its main doctrine, mother of all the rest, is a radical monotheism and a rejection of all idolatrous behavior, even those that might appear idolatrous. In order to avoid ornamental images that could lead to their worship, the art of the arabesques was developed for adorning palaces and mosques. Decoration is with letters or texts or with interlacing lines that surprise by their conjunction of monotony and beauty. Daily prayers are preceded by ablutions that reveal the value of water in the Islamic faith. Because it is scarce, it is a gift of God, and having it is a symbol of His generosity and abundance. That is why water has religious value and is present in their courtyards and gardens.

Within a few years after the death of the prophet Mohammed, in 632, Islam spread throughout the Arab countries and northern Africa.

The Koran

THERE ARE ONE HUNDRED fourteen *Suras* or chapters that all begin with the same phrase: "In the name of God, who is compassionate and merciful." Each Sura is divided in turn into *aleyas,* short phrases equivalent to Bible verses.

Tradition says that it was the archangel Gabriel who transmitted the content of the Koran to Mohammed. He did so in successive revelations, some in Mecca and others in Medina.

His illiterate condition is used as an argument in favor of the authenticity of its pages, because he would not have been able to write them, although another tradition indicates that he knew how to read and write. But it is said that these revelations were memorized by Mohammed and his followers.

At the end of his life, in the year 632, a successor called Uthman ibn Affan (another form of his name is Uzman; another Otman), who was the third orthodox caliph to govern the Islamic empire, ordered the compilation of the scattered texts and their grouping into what we call the Koran. Today the accepted text is the one sponsored by King Fuad I of Egypt, published in 1923 in Cairo, an edition that was based on the Eighth Century canonical text of Hafs ibn Suleiman.

The Koran sees itself as the ultimate revelation of God. It understands that, throughout history, God has revealed Himself to successive prophets, and His message has remained unchanged. For this reason, the Koran mentions Bible stories or acts of Jesus, but narrates them in a different manner. Abraham and Moses are

The Koran

outstanding figures; the story of Joseph is retold. It is said that during the time in Egypt the pharaoh beheaded Jewish males. For Islam, the Koran's version of the Bible stories is the right one, because it was revealed afterward and corrects them.

Koran (*Al Quran*) means "recital" and has the meaning of a text that must be read or recited out loud. Its language is classical Arabic and is considered the very word of Allah and is therefore untranslatable. Translations into modern languages are for didactic use, but have no religious value and do not compromise the truth of the Koran. Its stories do not follow the chronological order of the events, but keep returning to subjects and characters that have been mentioned before. This makes it difficult to read, because the subjects return and do not conclude throughout the pages.

The greatest sin in the Koran—and in Islam—is "association." This consists of associating God with anything that is not Himself. It does not refer to polytheism, but to the idolatry of prostrating oneself before anything that is not Allah himself. This fault is the origin of all other faults, and it is impossible to forget that in the Biblical tradition the worship of the golden calf in the desert is also assumed as the founding sin of almost all the rest.

The Koran calls God Allah, which is a way of naming the same Christian and Jewish God. The history of the word reveals that identity: in Hebrew, God is *Elohim*; in the Aramaic that Jesus spoke, it had been transformed into *Elah*; and in the Arabic language it became *Allah*.

Moby Dick, the White Whale

THE WHITE WHALE HAD torn off the leg of Captain Ahab, and he could not accept his fate. Like all whalers, he knew of the risk and the power of the whale when it is harpooned and defends itself with all its might. And Moby Dick was not just any whale; it was the largest and most powerful ever seen in the seas. Even so, Ahab could not contain his hatred and decided to go in search of the cetacean to destroy it and make it pay for the misfortune it had brought upon him. He dragged all those who went with him into his plan, sailors that only embarked in search of wages, unaware that in his thirst for vengeance, their captain was leading them on an insane adventure.

The interpretations of Moby Dick are numerous and varied. Like all good literature, it delves into external and internal reality, and ventures into the torturous paths of the soul and the entrails. "Not ignoring what is good, I am quick to perceive a horror. . .," muses Ishmael upon examining his wish to go to sea. It is a novel in which faith and the Bible are present on every page. From the names of the characters (Ahab, the most idolatrous of the kings of Israel; Ishmael, son of Abraham's slave; Rachel, who died giving birth to Benjamin; Elijah, the prophet) to entering a whalers' church in the port of New Bedford and the transcription of the sermon that the pastor preaches about Jonah and his stay in the whale. A sermon which could very well be preached today.

In my edition, the novel traverses nine hundred pages distributed over its one hundred thirty-five chapters. It has everything:

anguish, sadness, loneliness, love and horror; there is also friendship, courage and a sense of life shared. The Pequod, the whaling ship they man, is a symbol of the reduced space in which life is played out and where common fate is unescapable. That small wooden ship carries the life of the sailors who leave their loved ones on the shore and, from the very first day, they long to return to the arms of those who await them.

The end is foreseeable and uncompromising. After much sailing, they find the white whale and Ahab decides to discharge all his hatred against it. But evil cannot be defeated by more evil, however ferocious, and the irrationality of the cetacean vanquishes the captain's blindness. The whale destroys the ship, and Ahab drags everyone with him to death. Only Ishmael survives, who floats embracing a wooden coffin until a vessel rescues him. The epilogue evokes Job 1:16–19, when the four messengers say: "...and I alone have escaped to tell you."

Every metaphor has a second element that defines the first. "The sea *like a vast quicksilver mirror...*," says Rubén Darío. The novel *Moby Dick* is an immense metaphor, hundreds of pages long, in which life is like sailing in search of we are not sure what, but we do know that it lives among us. Its pages redeem us because Ishmael, like one resurrected, survived destruction and death.

Music and Dance

UNLIKE THE GREEK AND Roman cultures, which show naked bodies and exhibit them in statues and murals, Semitic cultures are modest and hide them. They include the Bible, for which "seeing the nakedness" of another was a serious fault and offense. Added to this is the First Commandment, which states: "You shall not make for yourself a graven image, or any likeness of anything that is in heaven above, or that is on the earth beneath, or that is in the water under the earth" (Deuteronomy 5:8).

The conjunction of the two elements was branded on the culture of Israel, to such a degree that not only did painting and sculpture not develop, but are foreign in essence. The prohibition of making images smothered all attempts at artistic expression through these means.

But the human spirit does not accept repressions and, if it cannot express itself in one way, it seeks to show how it feels in another. In the case of Israel, it found its way in literature, music and dance. We would now like to review the last two.

In the time of Jesus, we find that both expressions were present, adorning life and rituals.

In Matthew 26:30, after sharing the Last Supper, the disciples left for the Mount of Olives "singing a hymn," which may refer to psalms, in particular Psalms 113 to 118, called the *Hallel*, which means worship, and were sung toward the end of the Passover supper. At another time, when Jesus entered the house where Jairus' daughter already lay dead, the first thing we see are the flute players who, with their melodies, accompanied the suffering of the mourners (Matthew 9:23).

We are not certain of the difference between the "psalms and hymns and spiritual songs" referred to in Colossians 3:16 and Ephesians 5:19, where the Apostle encourages the churches to persevere with them. It is probable that the first are Bible psalms, the hymns are sung prayers and the spiritual songs are spontaneous songs of worship.

Revelation (14:2–3) describes John's vision and in it he hears zithers and songs, and in particular, a "new song" that he had never heard before. On the other hand, Paul and Silas sing hymns to God in prison (Acts 16:20).

As is to be expected from Miriam's tradition (Exodus 15:20), people also danced in Jesus' time. When Jesus tells the parable of the father who rejoices because his younger son has returned, he mentions a celebration with a feast where music and dancing abound (Luke 15:25).

The daughter of Herodias, Herod's wife, dances on the king's birthday, and she does it so seductively that the king is overcome by her movements and offers to give her anything she asks for. In line with that family's cruelty, she asked for the death of John the Baptist (Mark 6:21–25).

Song and dance were accompanied by noble instruments. The New Testament mentions, harps, cymbals, flutes and trumpets. Zithers had eight to ten chords and differed from the harp, which is smaller and does not have a sounding box. Cymbals consisted of two metal cones that were struck together. The flutes mentioned in Matthew 11:17 were made of reeds and had only one or two perforations, which gave them a monotonous sound suited for funerals. In the Old Testament trumpets were of horn, but in the First Century they were also made of metal. According to Revelation 8–11, there were seven angels with as many trumpets who announced the coming of Christ to reign on Earth.

Rabbi Regina Jonas
(1902–1944)

SHE WAS A RABBI when no woman had ever been one before. She remained in Berlin when almost everyone else was leaving. At 29 years of age she was given a book and the dedication said, "...to our first preacher since Deborah... who is not only a talented speaker but a good preacher, and with a sense of humor as well...." We can imagine the congregation smiling, happy with the rabbi that made them open up body and soul with her words.

She was one in millions, and even so, we wished to forget her. She left a text, a single text that survived a fire and was not reduced to ashes. In it she says that a woman could be a rabbi, and that she would be one, if the Lord called to her to such task. When violence and Nazism were growing and becoming intolerable, she was offered to leave the city. She refused, because leaving the city meant leaving her community. She decided to stay behind to preach, and accompany those she most loved in their pain and anguish. The psychiatrist Viktor Frankl, who would know her later in an extermination camp, remembered her sermons. He remembered that in them she dealt with Talmudic and Biblical subjects, and encouraged the lives of her brethren. However, Frankl did not mention her in his memoirs. A woman who shared forced labor with Regina in 1941 said, "The veil of forgetfulness must be allowed to fall over her because everything she did was forbidden."

On November 3, 1942 Regina and her mother Sarah made a state-mandated statement of their assets: some old furniture and

Rabbi Regina Jonas (1902–1944)

a gramophone soon to be confiscated. Three days later they were both deported to the Theresienstad Camp. Two years went by and one of the many trains that went from Theresienstad to Auschwitz-Birkenau took rabbi Regina Jonas and her mother to their deaths. They both died on December 12, 1944. Her brother Abraham had died one year earlier in the Lotz ghetto. Rabbi Joseph Norden had written Regina a letter a few weeks before: "Don't cry... there is no sense in crying; it doesn't help anyone and has a negative effect on you, especially on your eyes, your beautiful sweet eyes."

Seventy years have gone by. What can I wish for you now, Regina? For you to have embraced your mother during the last minute, the last beat of your heart.

Elohim, Elohai, Allah, God

LANGUAGES ARE LIVE ENTITIES that change with use and the passing of time. If simple everyday words go through this process, why not the words that name divinity? At times we forget that what we call God is also a linguistic construction subject to transformation.

In our culture, which we have basically inherited from our Greek and Roman counterparts, it is curious to note that God's name comes from Semitic tongues. It is so because the Biblical faith was born in the Orient but developed and expanded in Western Europe. The most ancient name for God is found in the cuneiform writings of Mesopotamia; they are Sumerian and Acadian texts that call Him *el* or *il* or *ilu*.

We have already said that proper names like Dani*el*, Rapha*el*, Ar*iel* are theophoric because they incorporate the name of God in their structure. That singular form derives in Hebrew into the word *elohim*, which is plural and is probably left over from a time when Israel was polytheistic. But in the Bible, the word *elohim* is used as singular and corresponds to the generic name for God. In its generic condition it designates both the God of Israel and that of any other people.

Around Jesus' time, Hebrew had been abandoned in Israel in favor of another Semitic language, Aramaic. In that language, God is *Elah* or *Eloah*. It is singular and leaves no doubt about its meaning. In Mark 15:34, Jesus exclaims "*Eloi, Eloi,*" which is a form of this Aramaic word that means "my God." The word *Elah* is used to call upon the same God that used to be called *Elohim* in Hebrew.

Elohim, Elohai, Allah, God

Several centuries later, a very ancient tongue, older than Hebrew and Aramaic, spread through the Semitic peoples: Arabic. By the Sixth Century it was already a literary tongue, and the Koran was written in what would later be known as classical Arabic. In that language, the word *Allah* is the companion of the two former ones used to name God.

In Spanish we use the word "Dios." Where does it come from? Most linguists agree that it is an Indo-European word (that is, not Semitic) which in Indian Sanskrit is *dyaus* (meaning *heaven*), in Iranian *deva*, in Greek *theos* and, finally, in Latin "deus" or its previous form "dius" which gave us our word *dios*. There are those who believe that the Sanskrit *dyaus* (heaven) derives from our word "day," which is not completely improbable. If so, our word for God involves the idea of light and the immensity of the heavens.

The National Constitution, Article 15

IT IS UNUSUAL TO find poetry in legal texts. Dense and boring, they are written to be discussed in court, to fill files and to be invoked or passed over by lawyers according to whether they make their arguments blossom or wilt.

But in 1853 the legislators embodied in these words the vocation of dignifying each person, each human being who inhabits the world. To my ears, they sound like the best poetry, the kind that fills our spirit:

> In the Argentine Nation there are no slaves: the few that exist today are set free as of the swearing in of this Constitution; and a special law shall regulate the indemnifications resulting from this declaration. Any agreement to purchase and sell persons is a crime for which those who commit it shall be responsible as well as the notary or official who authorizes it. Slaves that are brought in any way shall be freed by the sole act of stepping on the territory of the Republic.

Three things are said in these few lines, and all three move us: that there are no slaves here; that buying or selling persons is a crime; and that whoever arrives in these lands as a slave "is freed" by the sole act of stepping on our home soil. This last paragraph was added in the reform of 1860.

The National Constitution, Article 15

History twisted and turned to get there, and was cruel to many. The Assembly of 1813 states that the children of slaves born after January 31 of that year were declared to be free.

In 1825, the University of Buenos Aires taught that slavery was a crime, based on the texts of Argentine professor and jurist Pedro Somellera. Ten years later, the teacher was changed and with him the bibliography, now using the arguments of Spaniard José María Álvarez, who said that a slave is "a man but not a legal person" and "may be sold, bequeathed and donated like any of the other thing in our patrimony." He adds, for our derision, that slavery "is approved in the Sacred Scriptures." By then there were new underhanded forms of slavery in these lands.

Today, Article 15 is practically a relic, brilliant and beautiful. But it needs to be there so that we do not forget that slavery has taken on other forms that must be fought. It crouches in the last room of the brothel; it hides in the container with immigrants, in the clandestine textile work-shops, in the child labor that crushes childhood, that unique jewel that all persons deserve to experience.

(From the *Constitution of the Argentine Nation*)

The Bible and Slavery

WE SHOULD NOT EXPECT a narrative constructed in a patriarchal society to present woman as equal to man, just as we should not expect a text from the Bronze and Iron Age to explicitly condemn slavery or the death penalty. That would mean reading the texts literally, without taking into account their cultural contexts and limitations, and then humiliate their contents because they do not express our current understanding of social and personal relations.

Every text is created in a particular context and we must understand its values and options as inevitable consequences of them being rooted in the culture of its time. To suppose that because with the passing of time the community of Israel and then the Christian Church recognized them as sacred texts, they should be exempt from human and contextual dimension, is to fail to understand that God always uses human language to communicate, with all its limitations and beauties. If it were not so, if He expressed Himself in a pure, celestial and inhuman language, devoid of our baseness, who would be able to understand Him?

Therefore, it should not surprise us to find not a single line in the entire Bible condemning slavery. We must say, in its favor, that neither there is a single line justifying it: it only refers to it as something given. What is more, on several occasions a good gesture is rewarded by providing the faithful person with slaves, as we see in Genesis 12:6, or the mention of the slaves that Abraham "bought with his money" (17:23), or to emphasize how blessed Job's life was, who, among other things, had "very many servants," although

The Bible and Slavery

it should be noted that when his family and property were restored to him at the end of the book, the restoration of slaves was omitted (Job 42:12-13). Thus slavery was understood to be a sign of blessing for the slaves' owner.

However, the fact that the Bible stories do not condemn slavery does not mean that it does not lay the foundation for eliminating it. We cannot over look, without distorting the Biblical message, that it was the cry of the slaves that moved the God of Israel to free them from that tragedy in Egypt and initiate a process that culminated with the gift of a land in which to live. Jesus does not explicitly condemn slavery, but He breaks the rules of urbanity and converses with women in the light of day, touches the impure sick, feeds the hungry and announces freedom for the unjustly imprisoned. The Apostle Paul was to say that among those who embrace faith in Christ ". . .there is neither Jew nor Greek, there is neither slave nor free, there is neither male nor female. . .."

It will take centuries to overcome this scourge, and there will be those who will use Scripture to justify slavery, as they did with violence and torture. But the Bible's message—starting on its very first page—introduced a contradiction to that thinking: if we are all created by God in the same way and in His image, some cannot be intended for freedom and others for chains.

John Wesley

The passion for sharing faith and hope in God took him so far that we know him as the one who went through life on horseback. In the 18th century, the horse was the equivalent of our automobile, and on it Wesley traveled the roads, preaching two and three times per day.

As an Anglican pastor, he sought to preach in the churches. But when they were closed, he did so in the countryside, on the street and in the parks. It was not easy for him at first, because he had been educated in the orderly liturgy of his church (which he loved and never stopped practicing). But, if necessary, he broke with customs and traditions.

At Oxford they did not understand that his desire to share his faith led him to question ecclesiastical and cultural forms. His friends were few but enthusiastic, and soon others called them "the Methodists" because of their detailed way of living their faith, prayer and study of the Word.

An ocean storm brought him near the Moravian brothers, who prayed quietly while the entire ship groaned. The vastness of the American colonies showed him the need to announce the gospel throughout the world, not only in his land. Being close to people led him to understand that poverty and ignorance were not the fate that God wanted for His creatures.

He loved the Bible, but perceived as few others that condition, which was already present in the tradition of Israel, that the text was there to be read out loud. This conviction made him contribute to making the Biblical texts more than a book of paper but rather words to be cast to the winds, a message to share and a means for approaching God's truth.

He had passion for the lives of others. He sought to be an instrument of God to reach everyone with the message of salvation, at a time and in a place where faith was reserved for educated people, who could move within straight and pure doctrine. He was not a physician, but he founded hospitals; he was not a teacher, but he promoted the founding of schools; he was not a financier, but he created a fund to help victims of usury. He called slavery a "detestable business" and, already advanced in years, contributed to abolish it in his own country and in the colonies.

It was not a Bible text but Martin Luther's prologue to the Epistle to the Romans that awoke in his heart the truth of salvation through Christ. The road is not new: the Holy Spirit that inspired Paul to write that letter, that later inspired Martin Luther to commentate it, that further on made someone choose it as the reading for the study group that night, that same Spirit led John Wesley, much against his will, to that meeting in a house on Aldersgate Street. There, in his words, he felt "his heart burn" as it never had before, and he received the certainty that Christ had freed him from his sins and death. From that moment his life would no longer be the same.

Sophia Campbell
and Mary Alley, Slaves

ON NOVEMBER 29, 1758, John Wesley wrote in his diary, "I rode to Wansdworth and baptized two Negroes belonging to Mr. Gilbert, a gentleman lately come from Antigua." The baptism was a result of the three of them having participated in Wesley's preaching and having a strong conversion experience.

Upon his return to the island of Antigua, in the Caribbean, Nathaniel Gilbert resigned his post in the local Parliament and began to preach the gospel among those around him: slaves who worked in his sugar cane plantation. After a few years, he formed a congregation of 200 members. Later, as is typically the case, Nathaniel Gilbert died. He was succeeded for a short time by his brother Francis, who followed this popular tradition, and also died. The community was left without mentors, without those who took it to the gospel.

The Bible has duos of famous women. There were the midwives Shiphrah and Puah in Egypt; Naomi and her daughter-in-law Ruth; the cousins Elizabeth and Mary, mothers of John and Jesus; Martha and Mary, the sisters of Lazarus who received Jesus in their home. Now we would like to rescue from the bottom of the barrel of history and add to this distinguished list, the slaves Sophia Campbell and Mary Alley.

We know little about them, so little that it is not possible to attempt a biography or even a short summary of their lives. We know that they had both gone to London with their master to hear the preacher everyone was talking about. We know that they were baptized there, and also that when the Gilberts died, without titles or pomp, they took up the conduction of the church in Antigua, a congregation of slaves who had discovered that the gospel gave them the freedom denied to them by the world. They were pastors and preachers; they celebrated the arrival of babies in the church and gave thanks at funerals for the lives of those who had departed.

These two slave women, during a time when masters and pirates had the power, led the mission and made it grow, and were bearers of the light that shines in the darkness.

The Spirit ordained that there would be no grave for Sophia and Mary. Their remains lay somewhere on the island, already part of new life. They are sugar cane; they are the wood of a pulpit; they are the infinite sand. Somewhere in the world where beauty floods everything, we can imagine the immense loveliness of Sophia and Mary.

The Crucified God

THE CRUCIFIED GOD IS the title of the book written by the theologian Jürgen Moltmann. The first German edition was released in 1972. It was translated into Spanish in 1977, and the Sígueme publishing house printed several thousand copies.

Some books traveled to Buenos Aires, and I bought one in 1979. It´s still in my bookshelf, full of notes and underlining. My signature is in its cover. Other copies traveled to El Salvador. One of the books was probably bought by one of the Jesuits who worked as a professor at the University of Central America, in San Salvador.

On the night of November 16, 1989, we know that one of these books was not in the shelves of the library because it lay on a table or on a sofa, as it was being read.

We know this because that night, a group of soldiers of the Salvadorean army, commanded by Cornel René Emilio Ponce, broke into the house were the professors were staying and brutally killed them. They were Ignacio Ellacuría, Ignacio Martín, Segundo Montes, Juan Moreno, Armando López and Joaquín López. Elba Ramos, in charge of domestic duties, was also assassinated, as well as Celina, her fifteen year old daughter.

They destroyed their bodies by brutally beating them, they axed their extremities, and shot them several times. Their skulls were parted and their brains were scattered all over the front yard. They were eight defenseless persons whose blood splashed all over the walls and the floor, finding its way through the cracks of the

The Crucified God

mosaics and to the grass. It splattered onto the upholstery, some furniture, and dyed their clothes red, until it reached The Crucified God that one of them had been reading that night.

Today this book is displayed in a glassed shelf in the university. Its presence is disturbing for its silence and for what is evokes: an inalterable document of cruelty but also of human love. In one of its pages Moltmann quotes Eli Wiesel in a passage of his work *The Night*. The scene takes place in a Nazi extermination camp where a man is contemplating hanging dead bodies, and before such cruelty he asks a person standing next to him: "Where is God?" And the other person responds: "There, hanging from the rope." For the tortured dead body was God´s body.

When Does Day Begin?

FOR THE ROMANS, DAY began when the sun came up. They did not divide the day into twenty-four hours, but rather counted twelve hours of light, between dawn and dusk. Because of this, the hours did not last the same, being shorter or longer according to the time of year, and they were assigned numbers: first, second, third hour, and so on. Night was divided into four watches that coincided with the four night shifts.

Sun dials, called *horologia*, were used for counting the daytime hours and knowing what time it was, as were water watches. The latter allowed water to fall into various vessels at a steady rate, thereby marking the hours. They were called *clepsydrae*. This system was used in the New Testament times and is reflected in many texts: the parable of the laborers in the vineyard (Matthew 20:6), where the first ones began working at around seven in the morning (the first hour) and the last ones at five in the afternoon (the tenth hour). In Acts 2:15, it is assumed that the disciples could not be drunk because it was "the third hour," around nine in the morning.

In ancient Israel, the day began at nightfall, a method that is still being used today in Judaism for religious reckoning. The day was counted from one sunset to the next. This is reflected in the story of the creation when it repeats ". . .and there was evening and there was morning. . .." That is because it follows the order of creation, in which it is assumed that night was created first and then day. By saying "let there be light" it is understood that darkness

When Does Day Begin?

had already been created (Genesis 1:3). In Israel, as in Rome, the day had twelve unequal hours according to the time of the year, as mentioned by Jesus in John 11:9.

It was Niparchus of Nicea, a Greek astronomer, who in the 2nd century B.C. proposed implementing a twenty-four hour day in which all days had the same length. For this, he took noon as the point of reference and called it the twelfth hour. By doing so, he established zero hour and the twenty-fourth hour at midnight. However, common folk continued to use elastic hours until the mechanical clock with a face was invented in the 5th century and placed in church towers and public buildings. Only since then have the hours been the same and have the days begun and ended in the midnight darkness.

Job and the Living Redeemer
For George Pixley

JOB SUFFERS AND DOES not know why. It is the worst of sufferings because there seems to be no reason nor justification if there can exist justification for horror. But only he knows the depth of his suffering, which is in his body and in his soul. First he loses his children and then his skin is consumed by sores: Job was wounded in his flesh and bone.

There are those who advise him to curse God and die. In the thinking of that time, the two things went together; in particular, because if everything came from God, He was responsible for all calamities. And who is interested in a God that enjoys making His creatures suffer?

Jorge Pixley showed us in a memorable book that the message of Job is even more than that. It is an accusation against those who hasten to say "there must be a reason" for such a thing to happen to you, an accusation against those who judge without knowing what is in the heart of the sufferer and say "you must have done something to deserve this fate." This argument, superficial and devoid of any mercy, is used to justify tragedies, imprisonments, tortures, disappearances, poverty, oppression, unemployment, gender violence and the abandonment of the elderly. A theology is created to justify horror. Job's friends tell him to repent because there must be a reason for all of this happening to him. And Job knows, deep inside, that he is innocent and that neither he nor anyone else deserves to suffer.

Job and the Living Redeemer

It is interesting to see that in the narration, Job knows and declares that there is someone who will redeem him from his pain. It is a pain with two faces: that of the unjust and incomprehensible loss of his loved ones and of his blemished flesh; and that of being falsely accused, of being suspected by his friends of having violated that which he did not violate. He tells them: "I know that my Redeemer lives" (Job 19:25), and that redeemer will defend him before God on the day he sees Him face to face.

The soprano will sing this line vigorously in Handel's *Messiah*. Jorge Luis Borges will repeat it in his short story *The House of Asterion*. We do not see Him; we do not know the day or the time. But we know that on that day the redeemer will rise from the dust and be on the side of those who were mistreated and humiliated.

That Bread and that Wine

BREAD AND WINE ARE the work of human hands. They are there from the sower and the miller to the hands that knead and the eyes that watch the oven. We can say the same of wine: the work of the vine grower and the industriousness of the winepress must combine for the must to become good wine, through the work of handy craftsmen.

In the bread and wine we have before us the hands of men and women; there are long days of work and the effort and joy of the harvest. They are anonymous hands, hands of believers and non-believers, of the faithful and unfaithful, the honest and the deceitful. They could be the hands of visionaries who yearn for changes or desperate hands of those who have no hope. Hands of those who have lost the ability to imagine or generous hands eager for horizons. The hands that made the bread and wine for the Lord's table are not holy hands nor the best hands; they are simply hands: they may be the most expert or the clumsiest; they may be beautiful and delicate or deformed by time and life. Jesus wished it to be so.

Because the bread and wine at the table are almost another form of incarnation; it is there that we can catch a glimpse of Jesus immersed in our deepest and darkest history. Those things represent everything that we are, and make us see how, by His grace, He transforms that disorderly weave of human wills into the bread of blessing and into the wine of abundant life.

All Loves Excelling

THE ALARM GOES OFF and she gets up to see the sun rise.

She marks the page to keep reading the novel tomorrow.

She prepares the chocolate because her grandchildren are visiting her in the afternoon.

A man sits and rests underneath a linden tree.

Another one looks at the sky focusing his telescope in search of a new star.

Another one mixes the color that she likes.

Another one thinks about Antonio Porchia.

She thinks about him and about how much longer she must wait for him to arrive.

At dusk a woman remembers those who have gone, and fills up with melancholy and sadness.

Another one calculates the weight of a piece of bronze and multiplies it.

Another one stops to look at a statue that looks cold but is warm.

Someone prepares the flowers to adorn the temple and gathers them carefully.

The teacher prepares her class.

The youth practices the piano.

There is a party on the corner because a couple decided to join together.

Others imagine a future different from the present.
Others eat together and sing the songs they like.
She protects her six-moon womb.

Two friends reunite after decades and their friendship remains intact.

A young woman draws near and caresses his head while he sleeps.

It is so because there is a Love divine, all loves excelling.

www.ingramcontent.com/pod-product-compliance
Lightning Source LLC
Chambersburg PA
CBHW071231170426
43191CB00032B/1308